THE MANSFIELD CREED

At Mansfield University, we develop leaders.

We accomplish this by focusing on the four core values that have been our tradition since 1912: *Character, Scholarship, Culture, and Service.*

CHARACTER

We believe in integrity. We act with honesty and respect toward others. We take responsibility for our actions and reflect on their impact on ourselves and others.

SCHOLARSHIP

We believe in learning. We use rigorous, responsible, and critical inquiry to understand existing knowledge, acquire and share new knowledge, and apply what we learn. Each of us is both student and teacher.

CULTURE

We believe in celebrating humanity. We enrich ourselves and others by sharing and exploring our similarities and differences. We honor the past as we invent the future.

SERVICE

We believe in helping others. We work with others to improve the communities in which we now live and will touch in the future. Knowledge invests us with the power to improve our world and the responsibility to act.

In 1912, our student body adopted the above words, emphasizing their order: "Character as the essential, Scholarship as the means, Culture as the enrichment, and Service as the end of all worthy endeavor."

Academic Calendar Summary
Fall 2011

University Meeting Days	Aug 25-26
Classes Begin at 8:30am	Aug 29
Monday Classes (Beginning 6:00pm and after)	Sep 02
Last Day to DROP Classes	Sep 03
Last Day to ADD Classes	Sep 04
Labor Day - No Classes	Sep 05
Last Day to Submit:	Sep 07

      Credit-By-Exam form
      Application for Graduation for May 2012
      Pass/Fail form
      Repeat of Course form

Last Day to Submit Incomplete Grades	Sep 23
Last Day to Complete 'Credit by Exam'	Sep 27
Fall Holiday - No Classes	Oct 17-18
Mid-Semester Grades Due 4:00 pm	Oct 21
Registration for Spring 2012 Semester Begins	Oct 31
Last Day to Withdraw from a Course	Nov 04
Thanksgiving Holiday - No Classes	Nov 24-25
Fall Semester Classes End	Dec 09
Final Examination Period **	Dec 12-16
Fall Commencement	Dec 17
Fall Semester Grades Due 12:00 noon	Dec 19

Spring 2012

Academic Review Board	Jan 11-13
University Meeting Days	Jan 19-20
Classes Begin at 8:00am	Jan 23
Last Day to DROP Classes	Jan 28
Last Day to ADD Classes	Jan 29
Last Day to Submit:	Jan 31

      Credit-By-Exam form
      Application for Graduation for December 2012
      Pass/Fail form
      Repeat of Course form

Last Day to Submit Incomplete Grades	Feb 17
Last Day to Complete 'Credit by Exam'	Feb 20
Spring Holiday - No Classes	Mar 12-16
Mid-Semester Grades Due 4:00pm	Mar 23
Last Day to Withdraw from a Course	Mar 30
Registration for Fall 2012 Semester Begins	Apr 02
Spring Semester Classes End	May 04
Final Examination Period **	May 07-11
Spring Commencement	May 12
Spring Semester Grades Due (12:00 Noon)	May 14

** Friday is reserved for make up if it is necessary for the University to cancel final exams

Mansfield University
General Education Plan

Foundations 12 cr.

First-Year Seminar 3 - cr.

Oral Communication - 3 cr.

Written Communication 6 cr.
- ENG-1112 - 3 cr.
- Advanced Writing - 3 cr.

Approaches 18–20 cr.

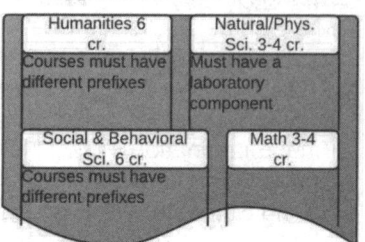

Humanities 6 cr.	Natural/Phys. Sci. 3-4 cr.
Courses must have different prefixes	Must have a laboratory component
Social & Behavioral Sci. 6 cr.	Math 3-4 cr.
Courses must have different prefixes	

Unity and Diversity
of Humanity - 12 cr.

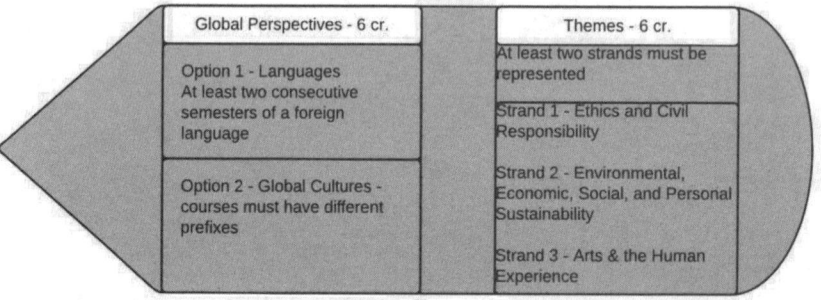

Global Perspectives - 6 cr.	Themes - 6 cr.
Option 1 - Languages At least two consecutive semesters of a foreign language	At least two strands must be represented
	Strand 1 - Ethics and Civil Responsibility
Option 2 - Global Cultures - courses must have different prefixes	Strand 2 - Environmental, Economic, Social, and Personal Sustainability
	Strand 3 - Arts & the Human Experience

Capstone

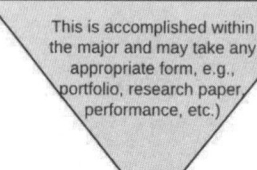

This is accomplished within the major and may take any appropriate form, e.g., portfolio, research paper, performance, etc.)

Academic Advising Help

See your individual departmental advisor or
Academic Advising Center
148 South Hall, ext. 4824
http://mansfield.edu/advising/

Admissions

Ground Floor South Hall, Ext. 4243
Graduate & Non-Degree Admissions/Enrollment - Ext. 4806
1-800-577-6826
http://admissions.mansfield.edu/

Athletic Mentoring/CHAMPS Life Skills

132 South Hall, Ext. 4825
http://gomounties.com/sports/2010/4/26/Champs%20Life%20Skills.aspx?tab=champ
slifeskills

Bookstore

2nd Floor Alumni Hall, Ext. 4921
1-800-577-6798
www.mansfieldbookstore.com

Campus Ministry

112 Pinecrest Manor, Ext. 4431
http://mansfield.edu/campus-ministry/

Career Center

Ground Floor Alumni Hall, Ext. 4133
http://career.mansfield.edu/

Counseling

Concerning family problems, depression, low self-esteem, substance abuse, etc.
Counseling Center
142 South Hall, Ext. 4695
http://mansfield.edu/counseling-center/

Computer/Network Issues

Campus Technologies
Ground Floor Memorial Hall, Ext. HELP (4357)
http://ct.mansfield.edu/

Dining Services

Manser Dining Hall
www.mansfielddining.com

Exercise

Kelchner Fitness Center, Ext. 4234
http://mansfield.edu/kfc/

Financial Aid

Returning Students
Financial Aid
224 South Hall, Ext. 4129

New Students
Financial Planning
134 Alumni Hall, Ext. 4878
http://esd.mansfield.edu/financial-aid/

First Year Experience

http://mansfield.edu/fye/

Graduate Studies

Ground Floor South Hall, Ext. 4818
1-800-577-6826

Greek Affairs

102 Pinecrest Manor, Ext. 4985
http://mansfield.edu/greek/

Health Clinic

Maple B, Ext. 4350

Housing

120 Pinecrest Manor, Ext. 4934
http://mansfield.edu/residence-life/

ID Cards

College Community Services (CCSI)
327 Alumni Hall, Ext. 4929

One Card
136 Alumni Hall
570-662-4074
http://mansfield.edu/onecard/

International Student Services

International Admissions/Information
Ground Floor South Hall, 570 662-4243
http://admissions.mansfield.edu/more/international-students/

International Exchange
110D Belknap Hall, 570 662-4603
http://mansfield.edu/international/international-student-exchange-program/

Job Search, help with resumes, etc.

Career Center
Ground Floor Alumni Hall, Ext. 4133
http://career.mansfield.edu/

Law Enforcement & Certification Programs

201 Memorial Hall, Ext. 4866
1-800-661-3640
http://cll.mansfield.edu/law-enforcement-programs/

Library Services

North Hall, Ext. 4670
library.mansfield.edu

Multicultural Affairs

311 Alumni Hall, Ext. 4381
http://mansfield.edu/multicultural-affairs/

Non-Degree Admissions/Enrollment

G22 South Hall
570-662-4408

Online Learning

Center for Lifelong Learning
200 Memorial Hall, Ext. 4244
1-800-661-3640

Orientation

Ground Floor South Hall, Ext. 4818
http://mansfield.edu/orientation/

Placement Tests

Enrollment Services
Ground Floor South Hall. Ext. 4818
http://mansfield.edu/orientation/placement-tests/

Police Services and Safety

Doane Center, Ext. 4900
http://mansfield.edu/police/

Registration Issues

Including add/drop, change of major
Office of the Registrar
224 South Hall, Ext. 4202
http://esd.mansfield.edu/registrar/

Residence Hall/Residence Life Issues

120 Pinecrest Manor, Ext. 4934

Residence Hall Technology Services

Pinecrest Ext. 5806 (Off campus, Dial 570-513-5806)
http://mansfield.edu/residence-life/

Right to Know Policy

Human Resources
118 Alumni Hall
http://mansfield.edu/hr/media/files/MU%20Right-to-
Know%20Policy%2012%2019%202008.pdf

Sports Camps

G13 Decker Gym, Ext. 4636
http://www.gomounties.com/sports/2011/1/31/GEN_0131111844.aspx?id=78

Student Accounts, Refunds, Balances

224 South Hall, Ext. 4888
http://esd.mansfield.edu/student-accounts/

Student Activities

324 Alumni Hall, Ext. 4983
http://mansfield.edu/student-affairs/student-activities/

Student Support Services

http://mansfield.edu/sss/

SUPPORT (Minority Mentoring Resource)

148 South Hall, Ext. 4824
http://catalog.mansfield.edu/content.php?catoid=11&navoid=233

Summer School

Ground Floor South Hall, Ext. 4818
http://mansfield.edu/summer/

Telephone/Voice Mail Issues

Campus Technologies
Ground Floor Memorial Hall, Ext. HELP (4357)
http://ct.mansfield.edu/

Transfer Credits

Admissions, Ground Floor South Hall, Ext. 4245
http://admissions.mansfield.edu/more/transfer-students/

Transcripts

Office of the Registrar
224 South Hall, Ext. 4202
http://esd.mansfield.edu/registrar/transcript-request/

Tutoring

Learning Center
143 South Hall, Ext. 4436

Veterans Benefits

New Student Financial Planning
134 Alumni Hall, Ext. 4418

Bibliography (APA Style)

What is a bibliography?

A bibliography is a list of sources used in compiling a document. You should arrange the bibliography in alphabetical order by the author's last name or, if there is no author, by the first main word of the title. You can ignore "A," "And," and "The" in a title.

There are several bibliographic styles, and your instructor may prefer a specific one. Be sure to find out which style you should use. Don't mix styles because you may confuse your reader. **The examples in this bibliography are written in the American Psychological Association (APA) style, which is commonly used in psychology and other social sciences.**

Examples

Below are example entries for different kinds of materials you might need to include in a bibliography.

A BOOK WITH ONE AUTHOR
Zambroski, R. (1959). *Sarah Akhtar: a biography*. New York: Five Lakes Publishing.

A BOOK WITH TWO OR MORE AUTHORS
Abbar, A., & Hightower, K. (2000). *Photographic essays of the end of a century*. Atlanta: Lakes & Sons.

A BOOK WITH AN EDITOR
Chor, A. (Ed.). (1991). *Writing clearly: Bullets, white space and common sense*. New York: Scootney Publishing.

A TRANSLATION OF A BOOK
Ben-Sachar, I. (1939). *Nunummy Nibh*. (J. Tippett and C. Polard, Trans.) Boston: Jean-Paul Deloria.

AN ANONYMOUS BOOK
Merriam-Webster's collegiate dictionary (10th ed.). (1993). Springfield, MA: Merriam-Webster.

A WORK IN MORE THAN ONE VOLUME
Greenberg, R. (1961). *Myth in children's literature* (Vols. 1-2). Boston: Ramona Publishing.

A SIGNED ARTICLE IN A JOURNAL
Con, A. (1984). The effect of pesticides on air quality. *Consolidated Messenger, 20*, 44-60.

A SIGNED ARTICLE IN A MONTHLY MAGAZINE
Shelly, D. B. (1995, March). Hardware innovations. *Awesome Computers*, 14-17.

A SIGNED ARTICLE IN A DAILY NEWSPAPER
Mughal, S. (1994, December 27). Speculation and development. *Island Hopper News*, p. D1.

AN UNSIGNED ARTICLE
The role of weather in economics. (1981, December 14). *Kimball Museum of Science Journal*, 16-21.

AN ENTRY IN AN ENCYCLOPEDIA
Ralph, B. (2000). Theseus. In *Encyclopedia of myth and legend*. (2000 ed., pp. 390-391). New York: Oxford University Press.

A BROCHURE (CORPORATE AUTHOR)
People for the Ethical Treatment of Animals (PETA). (1999). *PETA guidelines for the health and well-being of mammals* (2nd Ed.) [Brochure]. Kirkland, WA: Author.

The rules for creating an APA-style bibliography are:

- Double-space all entries *(the examples on this sheet are single-spaced to save space)*

- Use hanging indent paragraph style (align the first line with the left margin, and indent all subsequent lines .5 inches from the left margin).

- Type all authors' names with the last name first, separated by a comma. Use only initials for the first and middle names, and an ampersand (&) rather than "and" before the last author's name.

- In titles of books and articles, begin only the first word of each title, subtitle, and proper name with a capital letter. In the titles of journals, begin all significant words with a capital letter.

- Use italics or underlines for the titles of books and periodicals.

- Do not underline or use quotation marks around the titles of periodical articles.

- Give the full names of publishers, excluding "Co.," "Inc.," and the like.

- Use the abbreviation "p." or "pp." before page numbers in books, magazines, and newspapers, but not for scholarly journals.

- Separate each portion of each bibliography entry with a period followed by one space.

A GOVERNMENT DOCUMENT
U.S. Census Bureau. (1935). *Median gross pig fatality by counties of the United States, 1930*. (National Agriculture Statistic Service Publication No. 95905). Washington, DC: U.S. Government Printing Office.

COMPUTER SOFTWARE
Miller, M. E. (1993). The Interactive Tester (Version 4.0) [Computer software]. Westminster, CA: Psytek Services.

A FILM OR VIDEOTAPE
Sherman, M. (Producer), & Castaneda, M. A. (Supervising Director). (1937). *Mom's kitchen* [Videotape]. (Available from: School of Fine Art, 500 Aurora Avenue North, Burbank, CA 90210)

A PUBLISHED OR BROADCAST INTERVIEW
There is no approved style for interviews. You may cite an interview within the text as a personal communication.

A DOCUMENT ON THE INTERNET
Premier Music Online. (n.d.). *Persian style*. Retrieved August 23, 2004, from http://www.premier.us/archives/200408/23/perstyle.html

AN ARTICLE FROM AN ONLINE MAGAZINE OR JOURNAL (ACCESSED DIRECTLY)
Chaplin, H. (1999, February 19). Epidemic of extravagance. *Salon*. Retrieved July 13, 1999, from http://ww1.salon.com/money/1999/02/19chap.html

 **nnotated bibliography**

While a bibliography provides readers with the basic details of a source (author, title, publication date), an annotated bibliography adds a summary, or annotation, below each source. This summary includes a few phrases about the work and provides enough information so readers will understand the source's purpose, context and value within the paper. Begin each phrase with a capital and end with a period, even if it is not grammatically a complete sentence.

HOW TO WRITE AN ANNOTATED BIBLIOGRAPHY:

1 Locate sources (books, periodicals, documents, etc.) that may contain useful information or different perspectives on your topic.

2 Cite the source using the APA reference style.

3 On the lines following the source information, briefly summarize the document (in 150 words or less) doing one or more of the following:

- Describe the source content, purpose or central theme
- Note the relevance of the information and the authority or background of the author
- Indicate the intended audience
- Explain anything that makes this source unique
- Make readers aware of any weakness or bias

 **xamples**

Wesolowski, J. (1999). *Mother Teresa: a biography*. New York: Five Mile Publishing.

I got all the facts about Mother Teresa's life from this book. From the time she was 12 years old, Mother Teresa (born Agnes Gonxha Bojaxhiu) knew she had to be a missionary to spread the love of Christ. She is most well known for her devotion and service to the poor and disaster-stricken, and for founding the religious order, "The Missionaries of Charity." The author is very readable and includes a detailed bibliography.

Buttrick, D.B. (1995, March). Hardware innovations. *Awesome computers*, 7-13.

In analyzing the great debate between Mac and PC computers, this article helped me gather facts on each side's innovations. While PCs have a larger hold on the "at home" market, Macs have quickly gained status in educational and business realms. It seems the two camps have found a way to coincide in this industry by each dominating their own spheres—though which dominates their sphere the most is still at question. PC makers continue to develop cheaper, faster computers for home, office and gaming use, while Apple has developed faster, stronger computers that can easily handle high-resolution graphics and endless media formats. This article is unbiased in nature, letting the facts speak for themselves. It was helpful to see these statistics presented side-by-side as well as the different persectives offered by experts in the industry.

 School Specialty

Bibliography (Chicago Style)

What is a bibliography?

A bibliography, or "Works Cited" page, is a list of sources used in compiling a document. You should arrange the bibliography in alphabetical order by the author's last name or, if there is no author, by the first main word of the title. You can ignore "A," "And," and "The" in a title.

There are several bibliographic styles, and your instructor may prefer a specific one. Be sure to find out which style you should use. Don't mix styles because you may confuse your reader. **The examples in this bibliography are written in the Chicago style, which is commonly used in History and some humanities subjects.**

Examples

Below are example entries for different kinds of materials you might need to include in a bibliography.

A BOOK WITH ONE AUTHOR
Zambroski, Ray. *Sarah Akhtar: A Biography*. New York: Five Lakes Publishing, 1959.

A BOOK WITH TWO OR THREE AUTHORS
Burney, Chuck, Tyler Capriotti, and Ann Kovak. *A History of Aviation*. Toronto: Doubleday, 2004.

A BOOK WITH MORE THAN THREE AUTHORS
Silverstein, Gordon, William King, Gail Roth, Mia Jones, and Rena Clark. *The Eleusinian Mysteries*. New York: Penguin, 1999.

A BOOK WITH AN EDITOR
Faber, K. R., ed. *Shakespeare's Great Tragedies: Critical Essays*. London: Oxford UP, 1995.

A TRANSLATION OF A BOOK
Ben-Sachar, Ido. *Nunummy Nibh*. Translated by John Tippett and Carole Polard. Boston: Jean-Paul Deloria, 1939.

AN ANONYMOUS BOOK
The Chicago Manual of Style. 14th ed. Chicago: The University of Chicago Press, 1993.

A WORK IN MORE THAN ONE VOLUME
Greenberg, Richard. *Myth in Children's Literature*. 2 vols. Boston: Ramona Publishing, 1961.

A SIGNED ARTICLE IN A JOURNAL
Con, Aaron. "The Effect of Pesticides on Air Quality." *Consolidated Messenger* 20 (1984): 244-60.

A SIGNED ARTICLE IN A MONTHLY MAGAZINE
Shelly, Daniel B. "Hardware Innovations." *Awesome Computers*, 64 (March 1995): 7-13.

A SIGNED ARTICLE IN A NEWSPAPER
Mughal, Salman. "Speculation and Development." *Island Hopper News*, December 27, 1994, national edition, sec. D.

AN UNSIGNED ARTICLE
Anonymous. "The Role of Weather in Economics." *Wide World*, 14 (December 1981): 16-21.

AN ENTRY IN AN ENCYCLOPEDIA
Encyclopedia of Myth and Legend, 23rd ed. s.v. "Theseus."

The rules for creating a Chicago-style bibliography are:

■ Double-space all entries *(the examples on this sheet are single-spaced to save space)*

■ Use hanging indent paragraph styles (the first line of the paragraph is aligned with the left margin, and all subsequent lines are indented .5 inches from the left margin)

■ Type authors' last names first, with the last and first names separated by a comma, unless there are two or more authors. For references that have multiple authors, type the last name first for the first author, and type subsequent names with the first name first.

■ Type full titles and begin each important word with a capital letter.

■ Use italics or underlines for the titles of books and periodicals.

■ Enclose titles of periodical articles in quotation marks.

■ Type any publication information (place of publication, publisher's name, year, and so on) after each reference title.

■ The abbreviation "s.v." stands for "sub verbo" ("under the word") and is used when citing articles in alphabetically organized references such as encyclopedias.

A GOVERNMENT DOCUMENT
U.S. Census Bureau. *Median Gross Pig Fatality by Counties of the United States, 1930.* Prepared by the
National Agriculture Statistic Service, Census Bureau. Washington, DC, 1935.

A CD-ROM
Complete National Geographic: Wild Pigs. CD-ROM. Mindscape, 2002.

A FILM OR VIDEOTAPE
Sherman, Megan. *Mom's Kitchen,* VHS. Directed by Marea Angela Castaneda. Burbank, CA:
School of Fine Art, 1987.

A PUBLISHED OR BROADCAST INTERVIEW
Lance, Gail. "Alternative Truth: Interview with Gail Lance." By David Lumsden. *Hypnotic Monthly,*
(March 2001): 13-24.

A WEB PAGE
Kiyanfar, Alan. "Persian Style." *Premier Music Online,* January 28, 2003.
http://www.premier.us/articles/persian_style/ (accessed April 22, 2003).

AN ARTICLE FROM AN ONLINE MAGAZINE (ACCESSED DIRECTLY)
Chaplin, Heather. "Epidemic of Extravagance." *Salon,* February 19, 1999.
http://ww1.salon.com/money/1999/02/19chap.html (accessed July 12, 2000).

nnotated Bibliography

While a bibliography provides readers with the basic details of a source (author, title, publication date),
an annotated bibliography adds a summary, or annotation, below each source. This summary includes
a few phrases about the work and provides enough information so readers will understand the source's
purpose, context and value within the paper. Begin each phrase with a capital and end with a period,
even if it is not grammatically a complete sentence.

HOW TO WRITE AN ANNOTATED BIBLIOGRAPHY:

1 Locate sources (books, periodicals, documents, etc.) that may contain useful information or
different perspectives on your topic

2 Cite the source using the Chicago reference style.

3 On the lines following the source information, briefly summarize the document (in 150 words or
less) doing one or more of the following:

- Describe the source content, purpose or central theme
- Note the relevance of the information and the authority or background of the author
- Indicate the intended audience
- Explain anything that makes this source unique
- Make readers aware of any weakness or bias

 xamples

Wesolowski, Jonathon. *Mother Teresa: A Biography.* New York: Five Mile Publishing, 1999.

I got all the facts about Mother Teresa's life from this book. From the time she was 12 years old, Mother Teresa
(born Agnes Gonxha Bojaxhiu) knew she had to be a missionary to spread the love of Christ. She is most well
known for her devotion and service to the poor and disaster-stricken, and for founding the religious order,
"The Missionaries of Charity." The author is very readable and includes a detailed bibliography.

Shelly, Daniel B. "Hardware Innovations." *Awesome Computers,* March 1995, 7-13.

In analyzing the great debate between Mac and PC computers, this article helped me gather facts on each
side's innovations. While PCs have a larger hold on the "at home" market, Macs have quickly gained status in
educational and business realms. It seems the two camps have found a way to coincide in this industry by each
dominating their own spheres—though which dominates their sphere the most is still at question. PC makers
continue to develop cheaper, faster computers for home, office and gaming use, while Apple has developed
faster, stronger computers that can easily handle high-resolution graphics and endless media formats. This article is unbiased in nature, letting the facts speak for themselves. It was helpful to see these statistics presented
side-by-side as well as the different persectives offered by experts in the industry.

 School
Specialty

 Bibliography (MLA Style)

What is a bibliography?

A bibliography, or "Works Cited" page, is a list of sources used in compiling a document. You should arrange the bibliography in alphabetical order by the author's last name or, if there is no author, by the first main word of the title. You can ignore "A," "And," and "The" in a title.

There are several bibliographic styles, and your instructor may prefer a specific one. Be sure to find out which style you should use. Don't mix styles because you may confuse your reader. **The examples in this bibliography are written in the Modern Language Association (MLA) style, which is commonly used in the arts and humanities.**

 Examples

Below are example entries for different kinds of materials you might need to include in a bibliography.

A BOOK WITH ONE AUTHOR
Zambroski, Ray. *Sarah Akhtar: A Biography*. New York: Five Lakes Publishing, 1959. Print.

A BOOK WITH TWO OR THREE AUTHORS
Fernandez, Diana, and Andrew Janowicz. *Art Deco*. Atglen, PA: Schiffer, 1999. Print.

Burney, Chuck, Tyler Capriotti, and Ann Kovak. *A History of Aviation*. Toronto: Doubleday, 2004. Print.

A TRANSLATION OF A BOOK
Ben-Sachar, Ido. *Nunummy Nibh*. Trans. John Tippett and Carole Polard. Boston: Jean-Paul Deloria, 1939. Print.

AN ANONYMOUS BOOK
The Chicago Manual of Style. 14th ed. Chicago: The University of Chicago Press, 1993. Print.

A WORK IN MORE THAN ONE VOLUME
Greenberg, Richard. *Myth in Children's Literature*. Vols. 1-2. Boston: Ramona Publishing, 1961. Print.

A SIGNED ARTICLE IN A JOURNAL
Con, Aaron. "The Effect of Pesticides on Air Quality." *Consolidated Messenger* 1984. Print.

A SIGNED ARTICLE IN A MONTHLY MAGAZINE
Shelly, Daniel B. "Hardware Innovations." *Awesome Computers* March 1995. Print.

A SIGNED ARTICLE IN A NEWSPAPER
Mughal, Salman. "Speculation and Development." *Island Hopper News* 27 December 1994: D1. Print.

AN UNSIGNED ARTICLE
"The Role of Weather in Economics." *Wide World* 14 December 1981. Print.

AN ENTRY IN AN ENCYCLOPEDIA
"Theseus." *Encyclopedia of Myth and Legend*. 2000 ed. Print.

A BROCHURE (CORPORATE AUTHOR)
Smoking and Rats. PETA Guidelines for the Health of Mammals. Kirkland, WA: PETA Press, 1999. Print.

The rules for creating an MLA-style bibliography are:

- Double-space all entries *(the examples on this sheet are single-spaced to save space)*

- Use hanging indent paragraph style (the first line of the paragraph is aligned with the left margin, and all subsequent lines are indented .5 inches from the left margin).

- Type authors' last names first, with the last and first names separated by a comma, unless there are two or more authors. For references that have multiple authors, type the last name first for the first author, and type subsequent names with the first name first.

- Type full titles and begin each important word with a capital letter.

- Use italics for the titles of books, periodicals, films, etc.

- Enclose titles of periodical articles in quotation marks.

- Type publication information (place of publication, publisher's name, year, and so on) after each reference title.

- In using spaces after periods at the end of a sentence, be consistent and follow your instructor's advice.

- When no publisher name appears on the website, write N.p. for no publisher given. When sites omit a date of publication write n.d. for no date. For sources found only online (no print version) or on databases that do not provide pagination, write n. pag. for no pagination.

A GOVERNMENT DOCUMENT
U.S. Census Bureau. *Median Gross Pig Fatality by Counties of the United States, 1930.*
    Washington, DC: U.S. Government Printing Office, 1935. Print.

A CD ROM
"Marriage." *Encyclopedia Judaica.* CD-ROM. Vers. 1.0. Jerusalem: Judaica Multimedia, 1997.

A FILM OR VIDEOTAPE
Mom's Kitchen. Dir. Marea Angela Castaneda. Perf. Megan Sherman. Miramax, 1997.

A PUBLISHED OR BROADCAST INTERVIEW
Lance, Gail. *"Alternative Truth: Interview with Gail Lance."* Hypnotic Monthly. David Lumsden. Los Angeles:
    Brooms Inc., March 2001. Print.

AN ONLINE-ONLY PUBLICATION
Kessl, Fabian, and Nadia Kutsche. *"Rationalities, Practices, and Resistance in Post-Welfarism.*
    A Comment on Kevin Stenson." Social Work & Society 6.1 (2008): n. pag. Web. 10 Oct. 2008.

A WEB PAGE
Kiyanfar, Alan. *Persian Style.* 28 January 2003. Premier Music Online. 22 April 2004.

AN ARTICLE FROM AN ONLINE MAGAZINE (ACCESSED DIRECTLY)
Chaplin, Heather. *"Epidemic of Extravagance."* Salon. Web. 19 February 1999. 12 July 1999. No Print Version

Annotated bibliography

While a bibliography provides readers with the basic details of a source (author, title, publication date), an annotated bibliography adds a summary, or annotation, below each source. This summary includes a few phrases about the work and provides enough information so readers will understand the source's purpose, context and value within the paper. Begin each phrase with a capital and end twith a period, even if it is not grammatically a complete sentence.

HOW TO WRITE AN ANNOTATED BIBLIOGRAPHY:

1 Locate sources (books, periodicals, documents, etc.) that may contain useful information or different perspectives on your topic.

2 Cite the source using the MLA reference style.

3 On the lines following the source information, briefly summarize the document (in 150 words or less) doing one or more of the following:

- Describe the source content, purpose or central theme
- Note the relevance of the information and the authority or background of the author
- Indicate the intended audience
- Explain anything that makes this source unique
- Make readers aware of any weakness or bias

Examples

Wesolowski, Jonathon. <u>Mother Teresa: A Biography</u>. New York: Five Mile Publishing, 1999.

I got all the facts about Mother Teresa's life from this book. From the time she was 12 years old, Mother Teresa (born Agnes Gonxha Bojaxhiu) knew she had to be a missionary to spread the love of Christ. She is most well known for her devotion and service to the poor and disaster-stricken, and for founding the religious order, "The Missionaries of Charity." The author is very readable and includes a detailed bibliography.

Shelly, Daniel B. "Hardware Innovations." <u>Awesome Computers</u> March 1995: 7-13.

In analyzing the great debate between Mac and PC computers, this article helped me gather facts on each side's innovations. While PCs have a larger hold on the "at home" market, Macs have quickly gained status in educational and business realms. It seems the two camps have found a way to coincide in this industry by each dominating their own spheres—though which dominates their sphere the most is still at question. PC makers continue to develop cheaper, faster computers for home, office and gaming use, while Apple has developed faster, stronger computers that can easily handle high-resolution graphics and endless media formats. This article is unbiased in nature, letting the facts speak for themselves. It was helpful to see these statistics presented side-by-side as well as the different persectives offered by experts in the industry.

 School Specialty

Community Service Log

COMMSERL-08A1M

NAME OF STUDENT

GRADE

TEAM

SCHOOL

SCHOOL TEL. #

SERVICE AT

TEL. #

DATE

SUPERVISOR'S SIGNATURE

FROM　　　TO

TIME　　　TOTAL HOURS

DUTIES

SERVICE AT

TEL. #

DATE

SUPERVISOR'S SIGNATURE

FROM　　　TO

TIME　　　TOTAL HOURS

DUTIES

SERVICE AT

TEL. #

DATE

SUPERVISOR'S SIGNATURE

FROM　　　TO

TIME　　　TOTAL HOURS

DUTIES

SERVICE AT

TEL. #

DATE

SUPERVISOR'S SIGNATURE

FROM　　　TO

TIME　　　TOTAL HOURS

DUTIES

SERVICE AT

TEL. #

DATE

SUPERVISOR'S SIGNATURE

FROM　　　TO

TIME　　　TOTAL HOURS

DUTIES

SERVICE AT

TEL. #

DATE

SUPERVISOR'S SIGNATURE

FROM　　　TO

TIME　　　TOTAL HOURS

DUTIES

SERVICE AT

TEL. #

DATE

SUPERVISOR'S SIGNATURE

FROM　　　TO

TIME　　　TOTAL HOURS

DUTIES

eadership

"Teamwork can be summed up in five short words... we believe in each other."
- *Anonymous*

▶ Leadership is the **ability to motivate yourself and others** to accomplish a common goal through a **united effort.** Although there can only be one president, prime minister, or team captain, there are many others who lead by example. You are all the **leaders of your own lives.** Leadership develops through your **involvement** with family, school, and community.

LEADERSHIP QUALITIES

A GOOD STUDENT LEADER ALWAYS:

- Stays on top of his/her schoolwork ···➤ **IS RESPONSIBLE**
- Has a positive attitude ··➤ **CONVEYS OPTIMISM**
- Turns obstacles into challenges ···➤ **THINKS STRATEGICALLY**
- Simplifies even the most complicated tasks ································➤ **IS CLEAR**
- Sets personal and task priorities ···➤ **IS ORGANIZED**
- Encourages people to participate ···➤ **MOTIVATES**
- Takes a project through to its conclusion ····································➤ **IS DILIGENT**
- Relies on the support of others ··➤ **DELEGATES**
- Acknowledges the accomplishments of team members ·················➤ **ENCOURAGES**
- Earns the support of the team ···➤ **IS TRUSTWORTHY**

LEADERSHIP = PARTICIPATION + RESPONSIBILITY + STRATEGY

LEADERSHIP DEVELOPMENT

WHO is the most respected leader in your community?

List three of that person's achievements. Which character traits contributed to them?

WHY were the heads of committees for major school events chosen for those jobs?

What character traits did they need to perform their duties well? List ways in which you could develop those traits in your daily life.

WHAT is the most rewarding activity in which you have taken part?

Why was it rewarding? Did you work with others? What were their roles? List the character traits that were important for your success in this activity.

DEVELOP your leadership abilities.

Participate in activities that promote these positive traits and qualities.

REMEMBER:

Leadership starts with involvement! Get involved with your family, your school, and your community!

lass Schedule

SEMESTER / QUARTER

SEMESTER / QUARTER

TIME	CLASS /LOCATION		TIME	CLASS /LOCATION
		MON		
		TUE		
		WED		
		THU		
		FRI		

INSTRUCTOR / T.A.S

NAME	
PHONE	HRS.
E-MAIL	
NAME	
PHONE	HRS.
E-MAIL	
NAME	
PHONE	HRS.
E-MAIL	

INSTRUCTOR / T.A.S

NAME	
PHONE	HRS.
E-MAIL	
NAME	
PHONE	HRS.
E-MAIL	
NAME	
PHONE	HRS.
E-MAIL	

 School Specialty

*F*uture Class Planning

Most colleges and universities offer future class schedules. Obtain a copy of this schedule and list all the classes you might take in the left-hand column. Plan a tentative schedule in the center column. The right-hand column is used to record your actual schedule.

TERM ☐

POSSIBLE CLASSES	TENTATIVE SCHEDULE	ACTUAL SCHEDULE

TERM ☐

POSSIBLE CLASSES	TENTATIVE SCHEDULE	ACTUAL SCHEDULE

School Specialty

Multi-Cultural Calendar 2011-2012

In North America, many special days are observed and/or recognized. There are legal holidays, religious celebrations, special cultural days, and many more. The listings on these pages have been carefully compiled, and while Premier has attempted to ensure the correctness of these dates, we cannot guarantee complete accuracy. Please note that for some special days, the observance starts on the evening of the day before (e.g., Jewish and Muslim holidays). Some religious holidays are difficult to determine as these are based on lunar and astrological variables (esp. Hindu holidays). Your comments, suggestions, or corrections are kindly invited; please write to premier@premier.us

July 2011

Jul 1	Canada Day—Fête du Canada	Canada
Jul 1	NB, NS, ON, QC Confederation (1867)	Canada
Jul 1	P.E.I. Confederation (1873)	Canada
Jul 3	Emancipation Day	US Virgin Islands
Jul 3	Idaho—43rd State, 1890	ID
Jul 4	Independence Day (1776)	USA
Jul 5	Birthday of Guru Hargobind	Sikh
Jul 6	Dalai Lama's Birthday	Buddhist
Jul 9	Alaska Flag Day	AK
Jul 9	Martyrdom of the Báb	Baha'i
Jul 10	Wyoming—44th State, 1890	WY
Jul 11	Feast of St. Benedict	Catholic
Jul 13	Nathan B. Forrest's Birthday	TN
Jul 13	Obon (Ulambana)	Buddhist / Shinto
Jul 13	Ulambana (Obon)	Buddhist
Jul 14	Bastille Day (1789)	France
Jul 15	Guru Purnima	Hindu
Jul 15	MB, NT Confederation (1870)	Canada
Jul 16	Lailat al Bara'a	Islamic
Jul 17	Luis Muñoz Rivera's Birthday	Puerto Rico
Jul 20	BC Confederation (1871)	Canada
Jul 23	Birthday of Guru Harkrishan	Sikh
Jul 24	Pioneer Day (1847)	UT / Mormon
Jul 25	Constitution Day (1952)	Puerto Rico
Jul 25	Feast of St. Christopher	Catholic
Jul 26	Feast of Saints Joachim and Anne	Catholic
Jul 26	New York—11th State, 1788	NY
Jul 27	José Celso Barbosa's Birthday	Puerto Rico
Jul 31	Feast of St. Ignatius of Loyola	Catholic

August 2011

Aug 1	Civic Holiday	Canada
Aug 1	Colorado Day	CO
Aug 1	Colorado—38th State, 1876	CO
Aug 1	Dormition Fast (14 days)	Orthodox
Aug 1	Lammas	Celtic / Seasonal
Aug 1	Ramadan (1st day)	Islamic
Aug 5	Quds Day	Islamic
Aug 6	Hiroshima Day	Historical
Aug 6	Transfiguration of the Lord	Catholic / Orthodox
Aug 7	American Family Day	AZ
Aug 7	Friendship Day	Cultural
Aug 8	Victory Day, VJ Day	RI
Aug 10	Missouri—24th State, 1821	MO
Aug 13	Raksha-Bandhan	Hindu
Aug 15	Assumption of Mary	Catholic
Aug 15	Discovery Day (1896)	Canada (YT)
Aug 15	Dormition of the Theotokos	Orthodox
Aug 16	Bennington Battle Day	VT
Aug 19	National Aviation Day	USA
Aug 21	Hawaii—50th State, 1959	HI
Aug 22	Sri Krishna Jayanti (Krishna Janmashtami)	Hindu
Aug 26	Lailatul-Qadr	Islamic
Aug 27	Lyndon B. Johnson's Birthday	TX
Aug 30	Eid al Fitr (End of Ramadan)	Islamic
Aug 30	Huey P. Long Day	LA

September 2011

Sep 1	AB, SK Confederation (1905)	Canada
Sep 1	Ganesh Chaturthi	Hindu
Sep 1	Installation of Scriptures (Birthday)	Sikh
Sep 1	Orthodox New Year	Orthodox (East)
Sep 3	Revolutionary War ends (1783)	USA
Sep 5	Labor Day / Labour Day	USA / Canada
Sep 8	International Literacy Day	U.N.
Sep 8	Nativity of the Virgin Mary	Christian
Sep 8	Theotokos (Nativity of the Virgin Mary)	Orthodox
Sep 9	California—31st State, 1850	CA
Sep 11	Patriot Day (2001)	Historical
Sep 12	Defenders' Day (1812)	MD
Sep 14	Elevation of the Life-Giving Cross	Orthodox
Sep 14	Exaltation of the Holy Cross	Christian
Sep 16	Cherokee Strip Day (1893)	OK
Sep 16	Mildred Fish Harnack Day	WI
Sep 16	POW-MIA Recognition Day	USA
Sep 17	Citizenship Day (1787)	USA
Sep 18	Terry Fox Run	Canada
Sep 19	San Gennaro Day	Italian-American
Sep 21	International Day of Peace	U.N.
Sep 21	Wisconsin Day	WI
Sep 23	Autumnal Equinox (Fall begins)	Seasonal
Sep 23	Native American Day	WY
Sep 28	Frances Willard Day	WI
Sep 28	Navratri (9 days)	Hindu
Sep 29	Rosh Hashanah (Jewish New Year)	Jewish
Sep 29	St. Michael and All Angels	Catholic / Christian

October 2011

Oct 2	World Communion Day	Christian
Oct 3	National Child Health Day	Cultural
Oct 3	World Habitat Day	U.N.
Oct 4	Feast of St. Francis of Assisi	Catholic
Oct 8	Yom Kippur	Jewish
Oct 9	Birthday of Guru Ram Das	Sikh
Oct 9	Leif Erikson Day	Cultural
Oct 10	Oklahoma Historical Day	OK
Oct 10	Columbus Day	USA
Oct 10	Thanksgiving Day— Action de grâces	Canada
Oct 12	Dia de la Raza Latin	Latin American
Oct 12	Día de la Resistencia Indígena	Venezuela
Oct 13	Sukkot (7 days)	Jewish
Oct 15	Sweetest Day	Cultural
Oct 16	World Food Day	U.N.
Oct 18	Alaska Day (1867)	AK
Oct 19	Yorktown Victory Day (1781)	VA
Oct 20	Birth of the Báb (1819)	Baha'i
Oct 20	Installation of Scriptures (Guruship)	Sikh
Oct 20	Shemini Atzeret	Jewish
Oct 21	Simchat Torah	Jewish
Oct 24	United Nations Day	U.N.
Oct 26	Bandi Chhor Divas (Diwali)	Sikh
Oct 26	Deepavali (Dipavali, Diwali)	Buddhist / Hindu
Oct 27	Reformation Day (1517)	Protestant
Oct 31	Halloween (All Hallows Eve)	Cultural
Oct 31	Nevada Day—36th State, 1864	NV

November 2011

Nov 1	All Saints' Day	Catholic / Christian
Nov 1	D. Hamilton Jackson Day	Virgin Islands
Nov 2	All Souls' Day	Catholic
Nov 2	North Dakota—39th State, 1889	ND
Nov 2	South Dakota—40th State, 1889	SD
Nov 4	Will Rogers Day	OK
Nov 5	Bonfire Night (Guy Fawkes Night)	Britain
Nov 6	Eid al-Adha	Islamic
Nov 8	Montana—41st State, 1889	MT
Nov 10	Birthday of Guru Nanak Sahib	Sikh
Nov 10	Marine Corps Birthday (1775)	USA
Nov 11	Remembrance Day—Armistice	Canada
Nov 11	St. Martin's Day	Europe
Nov 11	Veterans' Day (Armistice Day)	USA
Nov 11	Washington—42nd State, 1889	WA
Nov 12	Birthday of Bahá'u'lláh	Baha'i
Nov 15	Nativity Fast (40 days)	Orthodox
Nov 16	International Day of Tolerance	U.N.
Nov 16	Oklahoma—46th State, 1907	OK
Nov 19	Discovery Day (1492)	Puerto Rico
Nov 20	Sir Wilfrid Laurier Day	Canada
Nov 20	Universal Children's Day	U.N.
Nov 21	Feast of Christ the King	Catholic
Nov 21	North Carolina—12th State, 1789	NC
Nov 24	Martyrdom of Guru Teg Bahadur	Sikh
Nov 24	Thanksgiving Day	USA
Nov 25	St. Catherine's Day	Cultural
Nov 26	Al-Hijra / Muharram (New Year)	Islamic
Nov 26	Day of the Covenant	Baha'i
Nov 27	Advent Begins (through Dec 24)	Catholic / Christian
Nov 28	Ascension of Abdu'l-Baha	Baha'i
Nov 29	Nellie Tayloe Ross's Birthday	WY
Nov 30	St. Andrew's Day	Catholic

December 2011

Dec 1	World AIDS Day	U.N.
Dec 3	Illinois—21st State, 1818	IL
Dec 6	St. Nicholas Day	Cultural / Europe
Dec 6	Ashura (Ashoora)	Islamic
Dec 7	Delaware Day (1st State, 1787)	DE
Dec 7	Pearl Harbor Remembrance Day (1941)	Historical
Dec 8	Bodhi Day (Rohatsu)	Buddhist
Dec 8	Immaculate Conception	Catholic
Dec 10	International Human Rights Day	U.N.
Dec 10	Mississippi—20th State, 1817	MS
Dec 10	Wyoming Day (suffrage to women, 1869)	WY
Dec 11	Indiana - 19th State, 1816	IN
Dec 12	Our Lady of Guadalupe	Catholic
Dec 12	Pennsylvania—2nd State, 1787	PA
Dec 13	St. Lucia Day	Scandinavian
Dec 14	Alabama—22nd State, 1819	AL
Dec 15	Bill of Rights Day (1791)	USA
Dec 15	Canada adopts Maple Leaf Flag (1964)	Canada
Dec 16	Boston Tea Party (1773)	USA
Dec 16	Mexican Posadas (to Dec 24)	Mexico
Dec 18	New Jersey—3rd State, 1787	NJ
Dec 21	Hanukkah / Chanukah (Festival of Lights) (8 days)	Jewish
Dec 21	Forefathers' Day	USA
Dec 21	Martyrdom of Guru Gobindh Singh's Elder Sons	Sikh
Dec 21	Winter Solstice (Winter begins)	Seasonal
Dec 24	Christmas Eve	Christian / Cultural
Dec 25	Christmas Day (Nativity of Christ / Noël)	Christian / Cultural
Dec 26	Boxing Day	Canada / UK
Dec 26	Kwanzaa (7 days)	Cultural
Dec 26	Martyrdom, Guru Gobindh Singh's Younger Sons	Sikh
Dec 26	St. Stephen's Day	Catholic
Dec 26	The 12 days of Christmas begin (Mummering)	Christian / NL
Dec 28	Day of the Holy Innocents	Catholic
Dec 28	Iowa—29th State, 1846	IA
Dec 29	Texas—28th State, 1845	TX
Dec 31	New Year's Eve	Cultural

Multi-Cultural Calendar 2011-2012

January 2012

Jan 1	Emancipation Proclamation (1863)	USA
Jan 1	Feast of St. Basil	Orthodox
Jan 1	Feast of the Circumcision	Byzantine
Jan 1	Gantan-sai (New Year)	Shinto
Jan 1	New Year's Day—	
	Jour de l'an	Canada / USA
Jan 1	Sol-nal (Korean New Year)	Korea
Jan 2	Georgia—4th State, 1788	GA
Jan 3	Alaska—49th State, 1959	AK
Jan 4	Utah—45th State, 1896	UT
Jan 5	Birthday of Guru Gobind Singh	Sikh
Jan 5	Twelfth Night Festival	Catholic
Jan 6	Epiphany / Three Kings Day	Christian
Jan 6	Feast of Theophany	Orthodox (West)
Jan 6	New Mexico—47th State, 1912	NM
Jan 7	Nativity of Christ (Julian cal.)	Orthodox
Jan 8	Battle of New Orleans Day (1815)	LA
Jan 8	Baptism of	
	the Lord Jesus	Orthodox / Christian
Jan 9	Connecticut—5th State, 1788	CT
Jan 9	Mahayana Buddhist New Year	Buddhist
Jan 11	Eugenio María de	
	Hostos Birthday	Puerto Rico
Jan 11	Sir John A. Macdonald Day	Canada
Jan 14	Maghi	Sikh
Jan 14	Orthodox New Year	Orthodox (West)
Jan 15	World Religion Day	Baha'i
Jan 16	Civil Rights Day	AZ
Jan 16	Dr. Martin Luther King, Jr. Day	USA
Jan 16	Idaho Human Rights Day	ID
Jan 16	Lee - Jackson - King Day	VA
Jan 16	Robert E. Lee Day (Observed)	AL MS
Jan 16	Wyoming Equality Day	WY
Jan 19	Confederate Heroes Day	TX
Jan 19	Feast of Theophany	
	(Julian cal.)	Orthodox (East)
Jan 19	Robert E. Lee's Birthday	AR FL KY LA SC
Jan 23	Chinese New Year, 4709—	
	Year of the Dragon	Chinese
Jan 25	Burns Night	Scottish
Jan 26	Michigan—26th State, 1837	MI
Jan 26	Signing of the Vietnam	
	Peace Agreement	USA
Jan 29	Kansas—34th State, 1861	KS
Jan 30	F.D. Roosevelt's Birthday	KY
Jan 31	Birthday of Guru Har Rai	Sikh

February 2012

Feb 1	National Freedom Day	USA
Feb 2	Candlemas	Orthodox (West)
Feb 2	Groundhog Day	Cultural
Feb 2	St. Brighid of Kildare	Celtic / Christian
Feb 4	Mawlid al-Nabi (Sunni)	Islamic
Feb 6	Massachusetts—6th State, 1788	MA
Feb 6	Ronald Reagan's Birthday	USA
Feb 7	Laura Ingalls Wilder's Birthday	Cultural
Feb 8	Boy Scout Day	Cultural
Feb 8	Nirvana Day	Buddhist
Feb 8	Tu B'Shevat (Tu Bishvat)	Jewish
Feb 9	Mawlid al-Nabi (Shi'a)	Islamic
Feb 12	Abraham Lincoln's Birthday	USA
Feb 12	Georgia Day	GA
Feb 14	Arizona—48th State, 1912	AZ
Feb 14	Oregon—33rd State, 1859	OR
Feb 14	Valentine's Day - Saint Valentine	Cultural
Feb 15	Candlemas	Orthodox (East)
Feb 15	National Flag of Canada Day	Canada
Feb 15	Susan B. Anthony Day	CO FL MN
Feb 20	Daisy Gatson Bates Day	AR
Feb 20	Family Day	Canada (AB)
Feb 20	Heritage Day	Canada
Feb 20	Louis Riel Day	Canada
Feb 20	Maha Shivaratri	Hindu
Feb 20	Presidents' Day	USA

Feb 21	Shrove Tuesday	
	(Mardi Gras)	Catholic/Christian
Feb 22	George Washington's Birthday	USA
Feb 23	Iwo Jima Day	USA
Feb 24	Día de la Bandera (Flag Day)	Mexico
Feb 26	Ayyam-i Ha	Baha'
Feb 27	Great Lent (40 days)	Orthodox

March 2012

Mar 1	Nebraska—37th State, 1867	NE
Mar 1	Ohio—17th State, 1803	OH
Mar 6	Town Meeting Day	VT
Mar 2	Texas Independence Day (1836)	TX
Mar 3	Florida—27th State, 1845	FL
Mar 4	Vermont—14th State, 1791	VT
Mar 5	Casimir Pulaski Day	IL
Mar 8	Holi	Hindu
Mar 8	International Women's Day	U.N.
Mar 8	Magha Puja Day	Buddhist
Mar 8	Purim	Jewish
Mar 10	Harriet Tubman Day	Cultural
Mar 12	Commonwealth Day	Canada
Mar 14	Nanakshahi Sikh New Year (Chet 1)	Sikh
Mar 15	Maine—23rd State, 1820	ME
Mar 17	Evacuation Day	MA (Suffolk Cnty.)
Mar 17	St. Patrick's Day	Cultural / Irish
Mar 20	National Agriculture Day	USA
Mar 20	Vernal Equinox (Spring begins)	Seasonal
Mar 20	Youth Day	OK
Mar 21	Naw-Rúz	Baha'i
Mar 21	World Poetry Day	Cultural
Mar 22	Abolition Day	Puerto Rico
Mar 22	World Water Day	U.N.
Mar 23	World Meteorological Day	U.N.
Mar 25	Annunciation	Orthodox
Mar 25	Maryland Day (1634)	MD
Mar 26	Prince Jonah Kuhio Kalanianaole Day	HI
Mar 26	Seward's Day	AK
Mar 31	Cesar Chavez's Birthday	Cultural
Mar 31	NL Confederation (1949)	Canada
Mar 31	Transfer Day	Virgin Islands

April 2012

Apr 1	April Fools' Day	Cultural
Apr 1	NU Confederation 1999	Canada
Apr 1	Palm Sunday	Christian
Apr 1	Ram Navami	Hindu
Apr 2	Pascua Florida Day	FL
Apr 4	Rev. M.L. King, Jr. assassinated	
	(1968)	USA
Apr 5	Booker T. Washington's Birthday	Cultural
Apr 5	Holy Thursday	
	(Maundy Thursday)	Christian
Apr 6	Good Friday / Holy Friday	Catholic/Christian
Apr 7	Passover—Pesach (8 days)	Jewish
Apr 7	World Health Day	U.N.
Apr 8	Easter Sunday—Pâques	Christian
Apr 8	Entrance into Jerusalem	Orthodox
Apr 9	Civil War ends (1865)	USA
Apr 9	Easter Monday—	
	Lundi de Pâques	Christian
Apr 10	National Siblings Day	Cultural
Apr 13	Thomas Jefferson's Birthday	AL OK
Apr 14	Khalsa Day—Vaisakhi	Sikh
Apr 14	Pan American Day	Americas
Apr 15	Pascha (Orthodox Easter)	Orthodox
Apr 16	José De Diego's Birthday	Puerto Rico
Apr 16	Patriots' Day (1775)	ME MA
Apr 18	Birthday of Guru Angad Dev	Sikh
Apr 18	Birthday of Guru Tegh Bahadur	Sikh
Apr 19	Yom Ha'Shoah	
	(Holocaust Remembrance Day)	Jewish
Apr 21	Ridvan (12 days)	Baha'i
Apr 21	San Jacinto Day (Alamo; 1836)	TX
Apr 22	Earth Day	Cultural
Apr 22	Oklahoma Day	OK

Apr 23	St. George's Day	Cultural / European
Apr 23	World Book Day /	
	Canada Book Day	U.N. / Cultural
Apr 25	Yom Ha'Zikaron	Jewish
Apr 26	Yom Ha'atzmaut	Jewish
Apr 27	National Arbor Day	USA / Cultural
Apr 28	Maryland—7th State, 1788	MD
Apr 30	Louisiana—18th State, 1812	LA

May 2012

May 1	May Day	Cultural
May 3	World Press Freedom Day	U.N.
May 5	Cinco de Mayo	Mexico
May 6	Buddha Day (Visakha Puja)	Buddhist
May 8	Harry S. Truman Day	MO
May 8	National Teacher Day	USA
May 9	National School Nurse Day	USA
May 10	Lag B'Omer	Jewish
May 11	Minnesota Day (32nd State, 1858)	MN
May 12	Florence Nightingale's Birthday	Cultural
May 13	Mother's Day—Fête des Mères	Cultural
May 15	International Day of Families	U.N.
May 17	Ascension Day	Catholic/Christian
May 19	Armed Forces Day	USA
May 20	Mecklenburg Independence Day	
	(1775)	NC
May 21	Victoria Day	Canada
May 23	Birthday of Guru Amar Das	Sikh
May 23	Declaration of the Bab	Baha'i
May 23	South Carolina—8th State, 1788	SC
May 24	Ascension of the Lord	Orthodox
May 27	Pentecost	Christian
May 27	Shavuot	Jewish
May 28	Memorial Day	USA
May 29	Ascension of Bahá'u'lláh	Baha'i
May 29	Rhode Island—13th State, 1790	RI
May 29	Wisconsin—30th State, 1848	WI
May 30	Feast Day of St. Joan of Arc	Catholic
May 31	World No-Tobacco Day	U.N. / Cultural

June 2012

Jun 1	Kentucky—15th State, 1792	KY
Jun 1	Tennessee—16th State, 1796	TN
Jun 3	Jefferson Davis' Birthday	USA
Jun 3	Pentecost	Christian / Orthodox
Jun 3	Trinity Sunday	Catholic / Christian
Jun 5	World Environment Day	U.N.
Jun 7	Corpus Christi	Roman Cath. / Christian
Jun 9	Poson / Dhamma Vijaya	Buddhist
Jun 11	Apostles' Fast (ends Jun 29)	Orthodox
Jun 11	King Kamehameha I Day	HI
Jun 13	Yukon Confederation (1898)	Canada
Jun 14	Flag Day	USA
Jun 14	Robert La Follette Sr. Day	WI
Jun 15	Arkansas—25th State, 1836	AR
Jun 15	Separation Day (1776)	DE
Jun 16	Trinity Test (June 16, 1945)	Historical
Jun 17	Bunker Hill Day (1775)	MA (Suffolk Cnty.)
Jun 17	Father's Day—Fête des Pères	Cultural
Jun 19	Emancipation Day (1865)	TX
Jun 19	Juneteenth (1865)	Cultural
Jun 20	Summer Solstice	
	(Summer begins)	Seasonal
Jun 20	West Virginia--35th State, 1863	WV
Jun 21	National Aboriginal Day	Canada
Jun 21	New Hampshire—9th State, 1788	NH
Jun 24	John Cabot Discovery Day	
	(1497)	Canada (NL)
Jun 24	Saint Jean-Baptiste	
	(Québec National Day)	Canada / QC
Jun 25	Virginia—10th State, 1788	VA
Jun 29	Feast of Saints Peter	
	and Paul	Catholic / Orthodox

School Specialty

eco’ resources
CONSUMERISM:
What’s the issue?

We buy a lot of STUFF!

Take a look around your room, or imagine it if you're not in it right now. How much of the stuff that you see do you use all the time? How much of it do you need? **How much of it could disappear without you even noticing?**

So, (why) do we buy all of this STUFF?

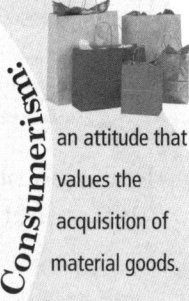

Consumerism: an attitude that values the acquisition of material goods.

1. happiness
Some people like to think they buy things because it makes them feel happy, satisfied, or cool. **But does it really?**

Think about it. Who or what is telling you that you'll feel cool, happy, and accepted if you buy a certain body spray, soft drink, or pair of shoes?

○ Friends   ○ Teachers

○ Family   ○ Advertisements

✗ Ads are flashy, funny, and appeal to our interests and emotions. Many advertisements hope to convince us that we're not quite good enough the way we are, but if we buy their product, we'll be a little closer to perfection.

Here are a few tricks of the advertising trade:
- Targeting emotions (acceptance, excitement, coolness)
- Repetition
- Celebrity endorsements
- Catchy jingles and slogans
- Not telling the whole story

Can you think of a print, radio, or television ad that fits each one of these advertising tricks?

How do you rate when it comes to consumerism?

	AGREE	DISAGREE
The last thing I bought was something that I wanted, but didn't really need.	○	○
I have most of the latest electronic gadgets.	○	○
Disposable cups and plates are great. They're really convenient.	○	○
Where or how something was made doesn't matter to me.	○	○
If something breaks, I'd rather buy a new one than try to fix it.	○	○
My room is full of "stuff" that I don't really use.	○	○

CHECKING "AGREE" TO ANY OF THESE STATEMENTS MEANS THAT YOU ARE BUYING INTO THE CONSUMERISM MINDSET.

Other **tricks** that corporations and advertisers use to get us to buy more stuff are

planned obsolescence
and perceived obsolescence.

2. planned obsolescence

Planned obsolescence is when products are **designed to be used up**, or become obsolete, within a certain time frame.

Some products are **created for obsolescence** through their function, like paper plates or machines with breakable parts. Other products, like clothing and shoes, become obsolete because advertisers tell us these items are no longer cool or fashionable.

Planned obsolescence is also sometimes known as: **"DESIGNED FOR THE DUMP."**

Objects Designed for the Dump

Paper towels

Fast food containers

Plastic cutlery

Greeting cards

Wall calendars

Plastic shopping bags

Airplane headphones

Mops

Computers

3. perceived obsolescence

In perceived obsolescence an object is still perfectly usable, but has become obsolete because it is no longer as **stylish** as something else.

Perceived obsolescence is part of planned obsolescence. When you go out and buy a new MP3 player, even though the only thing wrong with your old one is that it looks different, **you are buying into the concept of perceived obsolescence, literally!**

What are the last three things that you bought for yourself?

Why did you buy these items? *(Check all that apply.)*

○ They were replacing something that was broken

○ They were fulfilling a need

○ They were replacing something that looked old, but still worked fine

○ Other:

The problem is that besides being hard on our wallets, continually buying all of this stuff that we don't really need, and maybe don't even want, is **really hard on the environment.**

eco resources
CONSUMERISM:
What's the issue?

What does (me) buying STUFF have to do with the environment?

The things that you get at the store don't magically appear on the shelf. Everything that you buy, even your molded purple plastic MP3 case, is made out of natural resources and has to go through something called a **materials economy**, in which there are

5 STEPS: extraction, production, distribution, consumption, and disposal.

Materials economy: the rules and practices that guide how materials move from extraction to production to distribution to consumption to disposal.

1. extraction

In extraction, natural resources are collected for the purpose of creating a product.

No problem, right? Not quite. Many of the natural resources used to make the stuff we buy are non-renewable. That means they are only available in a limited supply—once we have used them up, we're out of luck. Even our renewable resources have limits. Trees can only grow so fast.

2. production

Once the natural resources have been extracted, they have to be refined, mixed with chemicals, and turned into the products that we all know and love, because let's face it: molded purple plastic isn't exactly something that you find growing naturally!

This step of the process is extremely **energy-intensive.** It usually results in air and water pollution, and creates a lot of waste.

Next time you see a big semi-truck belch out a stream of thick black smoke, or see an airplane leaving streaks across the sky, think about how much **energy and fuel are used up** at this stage of the process, and how much air and water pollution are created.

3. distribution

As soon as a product is created and cloaked in packaging, it gets crammed onto a truck, ship, or maybe even a plane, and is taken from wherever it was created to the store that we buy it in.

Did you know... ?

The waste generated while making a laptop is close to _____ times the weight of the computer.

a. 4   b. 40   c. 400   d. 4000

Answer: d. The Sierra Club reports that making a laptop creates an amount of waste close to 4000 times the weight of the computer.

4. consumption

This is the part where we drive to the store, shop around, buy our molded purple plastic, and then drive home again with our packages.

Consumption is the goal of the entire process and is the driving force behind it. The more we consume, the more that must be extracted, produced, and distributed for us to consume the next time we go to the store.

5. disposal

You contribute to this step of the process every day—each time you put something in the trash.

What are the last three things you threw out?

Object	Could it have been reused? recycled?	
#1: _____	○	○
#2: _____	○	○
#3: _____	○	○

Your particular piece of garbage might get dumped **straight into the landfill,** or could be incinerated before being dumped into the landfill. Either way it will be contributing to air, water, and land pollution.

So, basically, the more stuff you buy, the more energy you use, the more waste you create, and **the bigger your footprint or impact on the earth becomes.** And in this case, bigger is definitely not better.

1. extraction

2. production

3. distribution

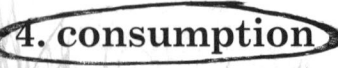

4. consumption

5. disposal

There is a better way! *The things that you do can make a difference. Where can you get involved in the process and start to make a change? Write your name beside the steps of the materials economy with which you are directly involved. Jot down something concrete that you can do in each of these steps to make a positive change.*

School Specialty

eco resources
CONSUMERISM:
What can I do about it?

Consumerism is a **bigger issue** than just figuring out what to do with all of the things you don't want anymore. It has to do with where the products come from, and the whole **attitude toward "STUFF"** that we have as a society.

Here are some things YOU can start doing today:

1. buy less:

- Share with or borrow things from your friends and family instead of buying them yourself
- Don't buy things that you don't need
- Avoid buying things that have been designed for the dump
- Send electronic birthday cards instead of buying paper ones
- Avoid single-serve pop and juice containers
- Avoid buying plastic or Styrofoam whenever possible

2. reuse:

- Start using a reusable water bottle
- Make wrapping paper out of old newspapers or magazines
- Pack your lunch in reusable containers
- Give your old clothing to a local charity
- Repair things instead of replacing them
- Create art out of broken or unusable objects

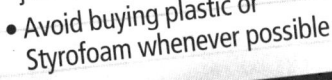

4. close the loop:

- Buy products made out of recycled materials

3. recycle:

- Before you throw something out, check to see if it can be recycled
- Recycle paper, plastic, and metal products

Recycle

Production

Consumption

Distribution

5. precycle:
- Buy things with little or no packaging
- Opt out of the extra packaging (tissue paper, ribbon, bags) that comes with your purchase
- Write a letter or send an email to the maker of your favorite product and ask them to cut down on their packaging

6. buy locally:
- Before you buy something find out where it's made—choose locally made products when you can
- Get fruits and veggies at a farmer's market

7. start a trend:
- Educate others about the effects that consumerism has on the environment
- Encourage your friends and family members to reduce their consumption

We are all consumers. What's important is that we become responsible consumers.

What do you think about consumerism?

AGREE DISAGREE

- ○ ○ I think that **consumerism** is related to a lot of **environmental problems**.
- ○ ○ The **culture of the country** that I live in revolves around **consumerism**.
- ○ ○ Convenience, luxury, materialism are things that I **value**.
- ○ ○ If people understood the **environmental problems** associated with consumerism, I think they would **stop buying so much** stuff.
- ○ ○ I should only be **buying the things I need**.
- ○ ○ I can significantly **reduce my impact on the Earth** by making a few changes.

The Shopper's Checklist
Before you buy, ask yourself...
Do I need it?

How many do I already have?

Is there anything that I already own that I could substitute for it?

How often will I use it?

How long will it last?

Could I borrow it from a friend or family member?

Can I do without it?

Will I be able to repair it if it breaks?

How will I dispose of it when I'm done using it?

Are the resources that went into it renewable or non-renewable?

Is it made of recycled materials, and is it recyclable?

?? What are you doing?
Put a checkmark next to each thing that you are already doing.

? What can you start doing?
Highlight the things that you will start doing today.

School Specialty

Cyber-smarts

Be cyber-smart!

Everyone has them—the friends who are always forwarding you corny jokes and chain emails, the ones who like posting embarrassing photos, the ones who IM things that make you think: "They'll regret that!"

Don't be one of those friends. Instead, **be sensitive, safe, and cyber-smart!**

Being sensitive in cyber-space is all about respect: **respecting others' time, privacy, and feelings.**

Respect their **time** by:

- thinking hard before forwarding jokes and chain messages
- double-checking those dramatic "Pass this on!" emails that may or may not be true, before passing them on; check an urban legends/online hoaxes website

Respect their **privacy** by:

- not forwarding an email unless you're positive the sender meant for others to see it
- using Bcc—"blind carbon copy"—when sending out group emails, so everyone's email addresses will be hidden (because maybe some people don't want the whole group to know their address)

Respect their **feelings** by:

- thinking twice before you post or send, about whether your message could hurt, offend, or anger someone
- doing your best to make sure your message can't be misunderstood (remember, people can't see your expression or hear your tone of voice for extra clues)
- knowing your "Netiquette"
- not posting or sending when you're angry!

Before you send or post, ask yourself:

- ☐ Am I angry or feeling sarcastic? Should I wait until I calm down?
- ☐ Would I say this to someone's face?
- ☐ How would I feel if I were the person seeing or receiving this?
- ☐ Am I sure my message can't be misunderstood in a way that would make someone hurt or offended?
- ☐ Am I positive I won't regret this tomorrow… or next week… or in ten years when I'm applying for a job and my possible boss Googles me?

R E S P E C T

Know your "netiquette"!

- Don't type an email using all capital letters (this is like SHOUTING!).
- Use polite, clean language.
- Remember that it's easy to be misunderstood, so do your best to be clear—and always be ready to explain or apologize.
- If you're joking, make yourself clear by adding a smiley. :-)

:-)   :)   ,-)   ;-)   :->   :-(

:<   :C   :-*   =:O   :-D

Think first... think twice!

Be Safe!

Imagine your private conversations being broadcast on TV. Kind of a weird thought? But is blogging or chatting online really all that different? The cyberworld may feel private, but it's really a public place... **so don't go public with your private information!**

Protect **yourself** with these important **DON'Ts** (and one **DO!**):

- **Don't share information that can identify you.** Even information like the name of your teacher or places you hang out can give clues about who and where you are.

- **Don't share photos,** unless you check with an adult.

- **Don't believe everything or everyone.** It's easy for people to lie online, or pretend they're someone they're not. Be especially careful about someone who wants to find out lots about you or meet you.

- **Don't arrange to get together with someone you've met online.** Remember that friends you meet online are still "strangers"; you just don't know enough about them to trust them completely. So do you really want them to know what you look like?

- **Do talk to an adult about anything that makes you unsure or uncomfortable.** It can be hard to tell an adult about something you've done online, especially if you regret it. But the sooner you tell, the better!

Being safe is mostly a matter of using your common sense. When in doubt... talk to an adult!

Protect your information by choosing and protecting your passwords with care. A good password is:

hard to guess
The best passwords are a combination of letters, numbers, and symbols.

not written anywhere
Think of passwords that you will be able to remember, but that others won't be able to guess. Here's one good idea: think of a sentence, and use the first letters of each word to create an acronym password.

only used for one thing
If you use the same password for different things, and it's guessed or discovered, all your information could be in trouble!

not shared!
Your friends may not snoop, mess up your stuff, or pretend to be you… but what if they record, lose, or share your password with someone who will? Accidents happen!

Remember, if someone has your password, he or she can not only access your information—but can even pretend to be you!

Protect your **computer** by:

- **Deleting suspicious emails or attachments**, including email from unknown senders, or attachments with extensions you don't recognize, like .exe.

- **Not downloading or installing software** without talking to an adult (like a parent or teacher). You could be downloading something that damages your computer, or "spyware" that collects information from it.

- **Disconnecting from the Internet between sessions**, to minimize the chance of any unintended "traffic" to or from your computer.

- **Backing up your files regularly…** just in case! Your family can also use anti-virus software and install firewalls to defend against viruses or hackers. It's also a good idea to disable the file-sharing option on your computer.

 **Be Smart!**

Cyber-bullies and spammers can really take the fun out of your online activities—**but you can outsmart them!**

Be smarter than cyber-bullies!

- **Don't respond**. Bullies are always looking for a reaction. If they don't get one from you they're likely to get bored and go off searching for other, more interesting targets.
- **Block the bully.** A cyber-bully can send you nasty messages a bunch of different ways, but he or she can't make you read them.
- **If you meet a bully** in cyberspace, leave that online environment. Remember, you can't be bullied if you can't be reached!
- **Tell someone.** Talk to an adult. Save the "evidence" (like hateful messages) to show them. Be sure to tell the whole story, even if it's tough.
- **Get active offline!** Hang out with your friends; get involved in sports and hobbies. No one can bully you online if you're too busy offline playing basketball with your friends.

Be smarter than spammers!

- **Keep your email address secret.** Spammers collect email addresses using spambots that troll the Internet looking for anything with an @ symbol in it. So if you post your email address anywhere on the Internet, you'll quickly find yourself getting loads of spam.
- **Pick an unusual email address.** Spammers also collect email addresses by guessing them, so get creative with your email address.
- **Don't reply to spam,** even to be taken off their list. If you reply spammers will know you actually read their emails!
- **Try a "white-list" spam filter.** These filters only allow you to receive emails from people you've put on your approved list.

What is cyber-bullying?

Cyber-bullying includes:

threatening: sending messages to scare someone

flaming: harassing someone by repeatedly sending them nasty messages

gossiping: spreading rumors or posting false information about someone

outing: passing along someone's private information

impersonating: pretending to be someone and posting messages as him or her, to damage his or her reputation

BE CYBER-SMART!

 School Specialty

Notes

Notes

TheSkinnyOn™

COLLEGE **SUCCESS**

JIM RANDEL AND CAROL RANDEL

The SkinnyOn™ College Success
COLLEGE & CAREER

TABLE OF CONTENTS

MAKING THE TRANSITION TO COLLEGE

hello...

You're on your own. You may still live at home; you may get daily phone calls from your parents to your dorm, but your education is now in your hands. There is even a federal privacy law (FERPA) prohibiting colleges from communicating with your parents about your progress unless you give your permission. It is a startling thought that there is no one to stop you from failing now. On the other hand, your success is all yours, too. Being a successful student is simpler than you might think. Follow these basic principles:

- BE THERE

- DO THE WORK

- GET HELP

- PLAN

- THINK

There it is—**college success in a nutshell**. All the pages that follow fall under one of the above categories. The extra benefit of taking responsibility for mastering these principles is that they will also lead to success in life.

BE THERE

Successful students go to class. It is the first and most simple rule for learning and getting good grades.

New college students are often unpleasantly surprised to discover that material presented in class is not a duplication of material in a textbook or handout. If you miss the class, you miss essential information. Even if you get notes from another student (which you should if you are absent), it is not the same as being there. Would you rather go to a movie or have your friend summarize it for you? There are attendance policies in all classes, and missing a certain percentage of class for any reason will usually result in a failing grade.

Being there **in body**, however, is not enough.

You must be an active listener and participant in order to get the most out of a class. A student who lets his or her focus wander to the scene outside the window may as well be absent.

Successful Students...

- Are prepared for class with pen, paper, books, and class material

- Are on time (professors get extremely annoyed at students who walk in after class has started)

- Pay attention

- Take notes

- Ask and answer questions

In college, **assignments** are an essential part of the course.

You're not in class all day, but you are expected to take on your own part of the learning by doing the assignments. Grades are largely based on completed assignments and exams that require semester-long study, not cramming.

Unlike in high school, assignments in college are not necessarily collected every day. Often, due dates are days or weeks in the future, and no one will be making sure that you are keeping up with the reading, or writing reflection pieces in your journal, or doing the research for your paper.

> The ways you will know that you have not kept up are when you fail a test, get an F on a paper, or get hopelessly lost as new concepts are added to concepts you never mastered in the first place.

Missed assignments will be reflected in your grade. They will also be reflected in how well you learn and remember the material. Keep in mind, college is for you. There is no point in being there if you are not learning anything.

GET HELP

College courses can be difficult. When students find the work very challenging, they tend to skip classes, stop handing in work, drop courses, or even leave school.

You can avoid embarking on the road toward failure by **seeking help at the first sign of trouble**.

All instructors have office hours. These are provided so students can go to their teachers for extra help when needed. Often, various departments provide small-group sessions such as recitations or math labs to practice concepts and skills.

Colleges have many services available that provide academic support for students. There are tutoring and writing centers that provide peer support and/or professional tutors to assist students in understanding the material and effectively writing essays and papers. Often, just having the material explained by someone with a different perspective is helpful. And one-on-one instruction is always a good way to increase comprehension.

There are many kinds of programs offered, often supported by federal grants, to help students succeed. The student handbook and your school's financial aid department will have a list of such services.

PLAN

Use your planner to account for how you will spend your time.

There are some commitments that are fixed, such as class and work hours. Most other activities are discretionary, though essential, and you must decide when and for how long you will do them. By scheduling time for study, exercise, social activities, meals, chores and sleep, you will go a long way toward ensuring your success.

THINK

You will hear a lot about using your critical-thinking skills in college. There is almost no need for the adjective "critical"—**just think**.

Time to come off of cruise control and engage your education. Start questioning all your old assumptions, judgments, and evaluations. Start creating new associations, connections, and conclusions.

If you leave college thinking the same thoughts you did when you entered, you have wasted several years of your life.

There is a reason you are taking all these courses you have never studied before. The reason is not to please your parents, the college administration, or even to enter some career. The real reason to learn is to grow.

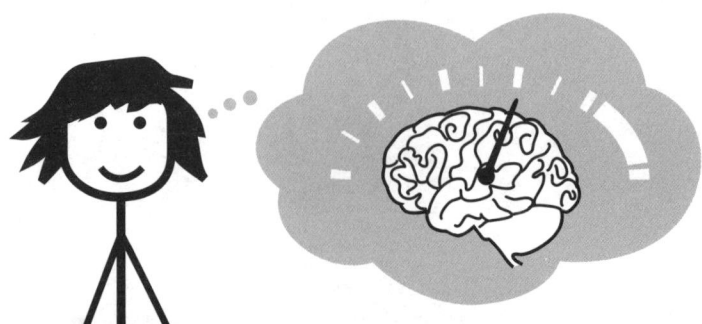

FIRST DAY OF CLASS

What is This Thing Called **Syllabus**?

They'll hand you one of these in every class on the first day. You will be tempted to stuff it in your book bag—and promptly lose it. Don't. It is your consumer protection plan, your instruction manual, your contacts list.

Your syllabus tells you:

- What the course is about

- The goal, objectives, and/or learning outcomes of the course

- What book(s) you will be using

- Class policies

- How to reach your instructor (e-mail address, phone number, office number)

- Your instructor's office hours

A course outline is often attached to the syllabus, showing the subject of each class meeting and the assignments for the semester.

Instructors do not look kindly on students who protest that they don't know how to reach a professor, or don't know what the assignment is, when it was on the syllabus.

Hang on to your syllabus. Put it in your class notebook for easy reference.

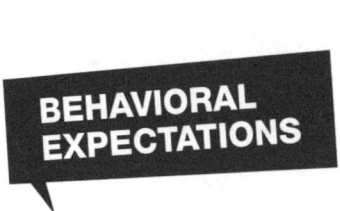

BEHAVIORAL EXPECTATIONS

Along with your syllabus, many instructors will list behavioral expectations for their class such as attendance and tardy policies. Reading these expectations carefully will keep your instructor happy. One of the expectations will be to turn off all cell phones.

There is no quicker way to make a professor **angry** than by texting during class…

…except by texting during a test—which brings up academic honesty/dishonesty policies. There are many ways to cheat in the age of technology. Your professor knows them all and has little patience for academic dishonesty. That includes cheating on tests, collaborating on assignments when not directed to do so, using work from one class for another class without permission, and using outside sources, including sources from the Internet, without citation (plagiarism).

Colleges have policies to deal with academic dishonesty, and they enforce them. They usually contain escalating consequences for each offense and end with expulsion.

> **The bottom line is:** Cheating makes no sense. It's your education—by taking shortcuts you are wasting your opportunities to learn.

Anyway, is being a cheater one of your goals for success in your future?

From the first day of classes you will be thrown in with all sorts of students, faculty, and staff. Unlike in high school, these people have no preconceived notion of who you are! This can be a wonderfully freeing feeling. **You can reinvent yourself.**

Were you the kid in high school who never spoke up in class? Even if you wanted to change your ways and start contributing, you may have resisted the impulse for fear that those who have known you for years would laugh at you. From the first day of class in your new environment, you can be that student who raises a hand when a question is asked.

The flip side of all this newness is that you can feel lonely or isolated—a stranger in a strange place. It is possible to get through an entire semester without knowing the names of the other students in your class. It's even possible to leave a class without knowing your professor's name (especially if you lost the syllabus that included his/her name and contact information). It is up to you to make connections with other people at school—and it's a good idea.

Learn his or her **name**!

HELLO, I'm **Mr.** _____!

- So that you can contact him/her for help. (School e-mail addresses are often based on names.)

- So that you can call him/her by name (professors get a warm and fuzzy feeling when called by name).

- So that you can get in touch with that professor in later years. When you need a college instructor's recommendation on an application for a job or graduate school, it's a sad shock to discover that there is no teacher you can turn to because none of them knew you. You never made a connection!

Many college professors want their students to be successful and will spend time to help them—**but only if the student asks**! The key idea here is that you must be the one to reach out. Go to your professor during office hours, ask questions, and make yourself known. Instructors are human (really) and will give the benefit of the doubt when it comes to grading students whom they see as sincerely interested and willing to make the effort to succeed in their classes.

CONNECT WITH OTHER STUDENTS

College is a place to form new relationships. Many people make lifelong friendships in college.

Many people find that future career success is enhanced by the networks they created with fellow students in college. Actually, socializing with people who were not raised in your hometown is one of the most valuable learning experiences college has to offer.

Making connections to other students also enhances your academic success.

Unlike in high school, college students are often encouraged to work with other students by forming study groups, which are a good way to learn material. Explaining concepts that you understand to students who are having trouble with them is a great way to reinforce your own comprehension. Working through material that you find difficult with students who have grasped the concepts is a good way to learn. Reviewing for exams with other students in the class is more fun, and ensures that you are making time to study, which will help you be successful in the course.

At the very least, get contact information from one student in each of your classes so you can get notes and find out what happened if you miss a class.

Boring! You have enough new books to tackle without having to waste time reading your student handbook, right?

Surprisingly, the handbook is full of useful information that may take months for you to discover on your own, or that you might never discover at all. Most handbooks are posted online so that you can refer to them at any time. Take the opportunity to check out the handbook at the beginning of your first semester.

There are things that you **need to know**, such as:

> Policies and procedures, including any penalties involved in breaking them

> Reference guide to services, clubs, activities, and academic advisors

> Locations of the career center, fitness facilities, financial aid office, campus employment office, the lost and found, and other areas

> Special programs and available scholarships

> Codes of conduct

> Ways to resolve complaints or file grievances

> Names of the president, deans, and other important administration, faculty, and staff

2 GOAL-SETTING

Psychologists distinguish between **external** values and **intrinsic** values.

External values are those dictated by others—society in general: the obtaining of money, power, respect, and fame. Internal values are more about you:

What personal beliefs are fundamental to who and what you are?

Studies have shown that when people put all of their energy toward obtaining goals founded on external values rather than on internal beliefs, the likelihood of goal achievement decreases. Yes, many of us want money, fame, power, and respect. But the pursuit of these goals must align with our most fundamental beliefs, or the probability of success is low.

> "People who seek a job purely on the basis of money rarely find either a satisfying job or the money they desire."
>
> ANONYMOUS

In other words, to be as **successful** as possible in achieving your dreams and goals, you cannot **divorce** your goals from your most basic values.

Thinking about how **you** define **"success"** will tell you a lot about yourself.

If you were to fast-forward twenty years, what would you want your life to look like? **That is how you define "success."**

There is no right and wrong answer about how you define success. There is nothing wrong with wanting material success. What's more, material and spiritual success are not mutually exclusive.

Do not be influenced by what you think others expect of you. Decide what success will be for you. Once you do that, you can then work backwards in crafting a plan from getting where you are today … to where you eventually hope to be.

"The great successful people of the world have used their imagination... they think ahead and create their mental picture in all its details, filling in here, adding a little there, altering this a bit and that a bit, but steadily building—steadily building."

ROBERT COLLIER, AMERICAN AUTHOR

Goal achievement is, to some degree, about **visualization**—about the ability to project an image several years ahead to see what and how you are living **"into the future."**

One of the great stories of achievement lore is that of Jim Carrey, who came to Hollywood from his native Canada with little more than a dream. He believed that somehow, someway, he would make it as a movie star.

And he visualized his success. In fact, to put real specificity to the picture, soon after arriving in Hollywood he wrote himself a check for $10,000,000 (even though his account at the time had perhaps $1,000) and postdated it five years.

As he wrote the check, he **visualized** himself going into a bank and cashing the check.

And here is the fun part. Because of movies like Ace Ventura: Pet Detective and others, Carrey was actually able to cash that check within five years—perhaps in large part because he was able to visualize his success and live every moment of every day working toward his picture-perfect day (cashing the check).

WHAT IS A GOAL?

Webster's Dictionary defines **"goal"** as:

"1. The line or place at which the race, trip, etc. is **ended**.

2. An object or end that one **strives** to attain, aim."

Although the second definition seems more like what we are discussing, the first definition is also important because it reminds us that a goal should be finite. **In other words, there should be an end date in mind.**

In order to create effective goals you need to be specific about what you are going to accomplish and by when.

Some people set vague goals (e.g., "to do better in school next semester"). Goals like that never seem to work. What does "better" actually mean?

A goal should be precise (e.g., "to improve my GPA to _____").

Similarly, a goal should have an end date (e.g., "by no later than the end of May, I will have _____").

If you want to maximize the probability of achieving your goals, you need to be precise as to exactly what it is you seek to accomplish and by when.

Adding **precision** to the equation helps your mind process what needs to get done by when.

There is no standard definition for a long- or short-term goal.

For purposes of this book, let's think of a short-term goal as an objective that can be achieved within one year, and a long-term goal as everything else.

You should also be careful about what you consider a goal. A goal is something you need to **strive** for over a period of time and that will **challenge you** to some degree.

Distinguish between a "**task**," a "**chore**," or even an "**obligation**." These latter descriptions are more appropriate to items you would put on a daily or weekly To-Do List.

One way to think about tasks and goals:

> "Tasks go on To-Do Lists; goals go on Mission Statements."

One other important point: Over time, people's goals change. Every six months or so, at least for your long-term goals, find a quiet time and space to reflect on them. Perhaps changes are in order. We also suggest writing down your goals—the act of writing imprints a visual image of achievement in your mind.

YOUR GOALS

There are no right and wrong goals. What is **important to you** is all that matters.

When you write your goals, it is a time to **let your mind fly**.

Forget for the moment what is practical, even perhaps what is realistic. Goal-setting is your time to "create"—at least on paper—your dreamscape, the ideal life you would like to live. In order to create effective goals you need to be specific about what you are going to accomplish and by when.

Consider keeping your goals to yourself. No one knows you better than you know yourself. If you open up to others what your long-term goals are, they may have comments that are not conducive to your achievement.

Many successful people (some of whom we presume wrote down their goals) were discouraged from pursuing something important to them by a parent or other person in authority. People like Elvis Presley, Paul McCartney, and Barbra Streisand were all told at one time or another that they should give up music— "what a silly waste of time" they may have been told. **Fortunately, they did not listen!!**

The most important thing to learn about goals is that thinking about them is not enough. Far too many people take the step of identifying their goals … and then just wait for them to happen.

Consider the old adage:

"Nothing great just **happens**."

What that saying means is that if you want something great to happen in your life, you are going to have to **make it happen**! Wishing, hoping, daydreaming, and even writing down goals, all that is nice,

but as Einstein said:

"NOTHING HAPPENS until there is **action.**"

Sooner or later you are going to realize that your life is in your hands, for better or worse. No one is going to come along and create the life you want. So, if you want to achieve your goals, you have to determine what steps are necessary to get from here to there and **start moving**.

Good News: Many people do not know the precise steps to take them to the realization of their goals. BUT, by moving forward, in the **DIRECTION** of their goals, they start to find the path—**or steps**—that takes them where they want to go.

3 TIME MANAGEMENT

"Time management" is an often-used phrase. But, what does it mean?

It refers to the collection of skills, techniques, strategies, and attitudes that allow a person to use time most **effectively**.

For each of us, an hour is 60 minutes or 3,600 seconds. But some people know how to make better use of an hour than others. Those who practice effective time management are more likely to achieve their goals and aspirations.

"Those who respect time the least are the same people bemoaning that there is not enough time in the day."

ANONYMOUS

Time is a fleeting asset. Simply acknowledging this is a first step toward making better use of your time.

On the other hand, time management is not about trying to maximize the productivity of every hour in your life. Life is a continuing balance between growth and achievement, and relaxation and leisure. Finding the right balance is one of the challenges we face in pursuit of a healthy life. In this chapter, we will help you identify what it is you want to do with the 24-hour gift we call a "day."

TIME JOURNALS

In order to get a better sense of how effective a time manager you may **(or may not)** be, you need to track how you are spending your time. A time journal can help you do that.

"Flying blind is one way of describing people who have no sense of how they are allocating their daily gift—the hours of a day."

ANONYMOUS

A time journal is nothing more than a diary. We suggest that at the end of every day for one week, you enter in increments of 30 minutes what you did in the preceding 24 hours. General categories might be:

1. **Sleep**

2. **Class time**

3. **Class preparation and study**

4. **Phone or text friends**

5. **TV or Internet**

6. **Recreation**

7. **Eating**

8. **Shower, dress for school**

9. **Exercise**

10. **Miscellaneous**

There is no magic to the categories or form of a time journal. The point is for you to see how you are allocating your most precious resource—your time. Preparing a time journal might surprise you. You might find that you are spending more (or less) time on certain activities than you should.

One way to improve your time-management skills is to get the most you can out of every classroom hour. Our advice here is pretty basic: The more energy and curiosity you bring to your class time, the more you will take from it.

Energy comes from getting enough sleep and developing healthy habits, including exercise and healthy eating. The more energy you bring to your class time, the more you will take out of each class. When it comes to time management, some experts say the discussion should not be about time, per se, but rather about energy.

If you want to achieve a lot in life, learn to maximize your energy. One energetic hour is more valuable than spending five hours just "going through the motions."

Most experts state that you need about **2 to 2.5 hours** outside of class for every **one hour** in class. These 2 to 2.5 hours are for tasks such as assignments, reading, studying, and writing papers.

No matter how you slice it, this graph describes school performance for **99% of the student body:**

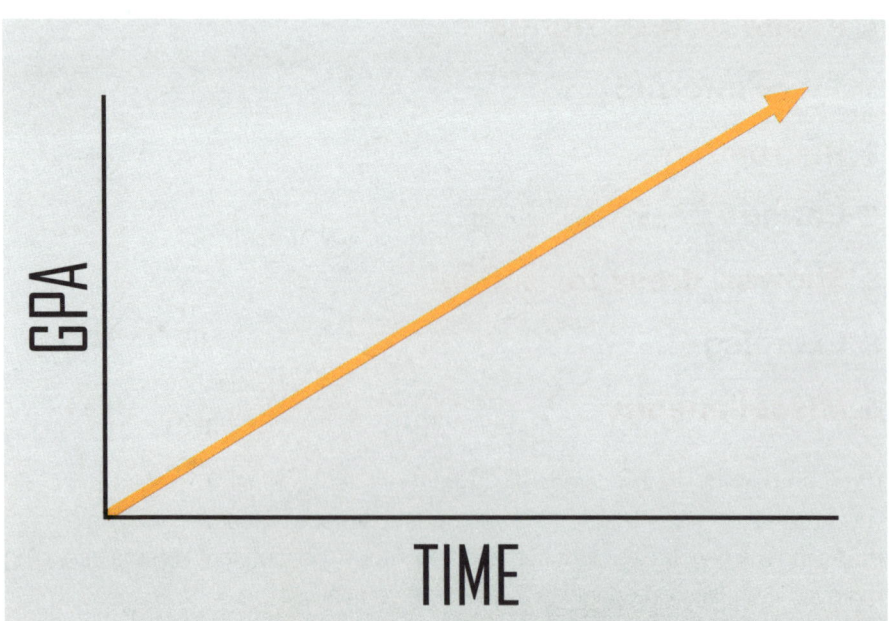

EVALUATE YOUR WEEKLY SCHEDULE

OK, now that you know you need 2 to 2.5 hours of time outside of class for every hour in class, you need to make sure it's feasible for you. So, if you are taking 15 hours of course credits this semester, you need to determine if you have **30** to **40 hours** every week to spend on tasks outside class time.

If you do have those hours available, an equally important question is, do you have the self-discipline to use those hours for schoolwork?

Most students have a lot going on in their lives. A large part of everyone's life is choosing among all the competing alternatives for each minute and hour, but we will get to that.

First, you have to be sure that you have enough space in the week to allocate for class time and outside class time. If you are taking 15 credits, then you need to have about 50 hours available to you per week for a solid performance in school. Do you have that? Refer back to your time journal. What other major obligations do you have? (Job, sports, family, etc.)

OK, other than school, my activities total 125 hours per week. But wait, I need 50 hours for school time … 24 x 7 = 168.

UH OH.

Balancing all that you have going on is a constant struggle.

If you want to accomplish your goals you need to find and guard the time you need to make them happen.

There have been several recent studies conducted on top achievers, including athletes, entertainers, and business people. A very small percentage of top performers succeeded through sheer talent, braininess, or athleticism. But most got to where they wanted to be through hours and hours of focused practice, preparation, and persistence.

Presumably, you have some goals for your years in school and for your years after school. Whatever your goals may be, you need to understand and acknowledge the **direct correlation between time invested and goal achievement.**

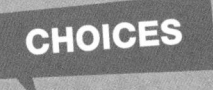

CHOICES

Now we've come to one of the thorniest topics in this chapter—**the need to make choices**.

The choices you make every day will affect your life and your future. It is not necessarily true that if you do poorly in school, you are destined to be a failure in life. Every person hits his or her stride at different times.

But, if you do not develop the ability to make good choices—now, right now—you may very well fall far short of not only your goals, but of your potential.

Often your decisions will come down to:

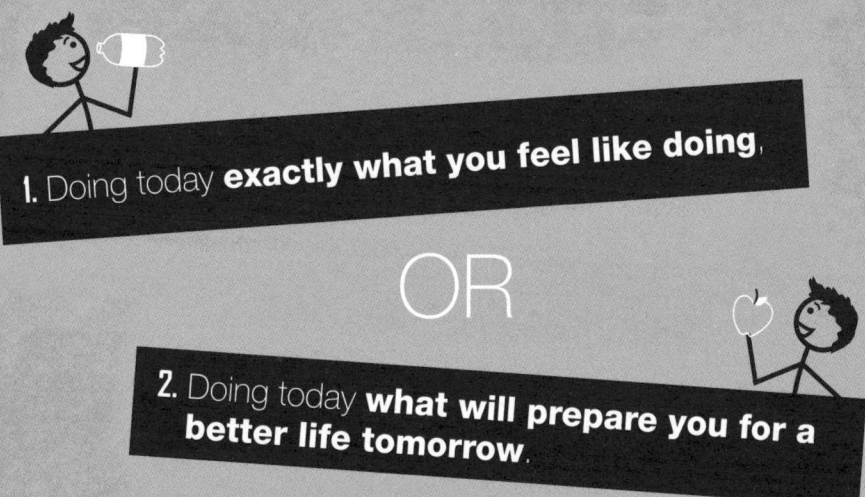

1. Doing today **exactly what you feel like doing,**

OR

2. Doing today **what will prepare you for a better life tomorrow**.

The choices you can make today—to do your best in school, to lead a healthy life, to treat others with respect and compassion—will not only prepare you for what comes next, but will also help you develop the habits and routines you will need in the competitive world awaiting you.

"Successful people do not enjoy doing the things that others do not want to do, but they do them nevertheless."

ALBERT E.N. GRAY

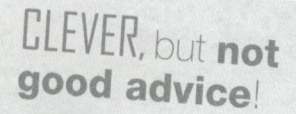

CLEVER, but **not good advice**!

Mark Twain said:

"Never put off to tomorrow what you can put off to the day after tomorrow."

Procrastination is the **enemy** of achievement.

Procrastination is the word we give the myriad of excuses we all have for putting off working at a project, chore, or challenge. Procrastination is just so darn easy.

Success in school and in life will depend upon your ability to take action. As Einstein said, "Nothing happens until something moves." If you want to move forward in life, you will have to defeat the urge to procrastinate.

Procrastination is powerful. We know from the law of inertia that a body at rest will stay at rest unless and until acted upon by an outside force. Inertia is a powerful force. But physics also tells us that a body in motion will stay in motion until acted upon by an outside force. So, once you do get moving, it will be easier to stay moving!

YOU MUST LEARN TO BEAT BACK **INERTIA**

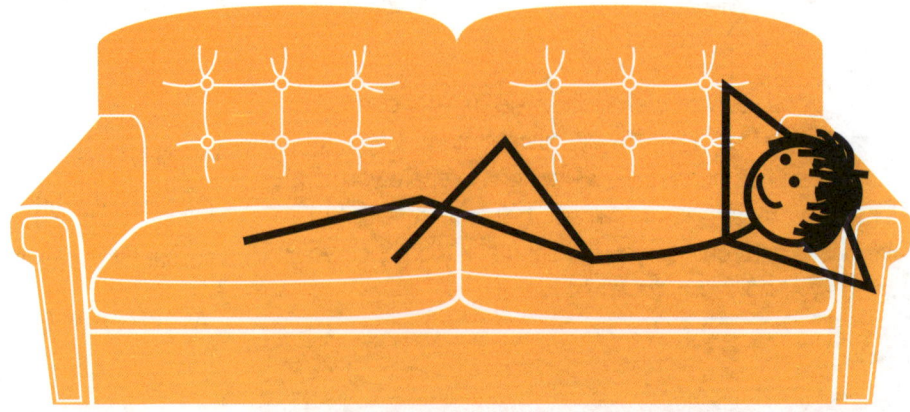

Prioritizing is about making choices between
two competing realities:

1. There are only so many hours in the day.

VS.

2. How much time you give to your goals will
directly affect your achievement.

We have already discussed choices and making the hard decisions that will
allow you to find as much time as possible to devote to your objectives. But, time
management is not just about isolating time. It is just as much about using the
time you have effectively. **That is what prioritizing is about.**

Not all activities are going to move you closer to your objectives. Some are going
to have more of an effect than others. Prioritizing means developing a sequence in
all that you have to do.

What should you do first, then second and so on—with the understanding that as the
day progresses, things may intervene that will prevent you from getting to everything?

Which activities are **important**,
not just urgent?

Which activities can be **delayed**
and which cannot?

Deciding, every single day, the sequence of what you will do and when is called
"prioritizing." And how you prioritize your days' tasks can have an enormous effect
on what you actually achieve.

Having the proper amount of time allocated to class time and outside class time is important, of course, but if you do not take advantage of those hours, you are just kidding yourself.

The **#1 determinant** for powerful and effective time management is FOCUS.

Did you ever use a magnifying glass to train the sun's rays on a leaf or piece of paper? When the heat from the sun is concentrated, it can light a fire. That's how to think of focus.

When you train all of your mental capabilities on a task, the heat and power of your brain power is concentrated. The result may be a fire—a kind of spontaneous combustion of creativity, problem-solving and substantive analysis.

As the enemy of action is procrastination, the enemy of focus is distraction. And like procrastination, distractions are so very seductive. You get the picture: you are sitting down to study and your cell phone rings. Or, you get a text message or e-mail ding. Or, someone drops in on you. GAME OVER. Your focus is gone.

If you want to get the most out of every hour, you need to prevent distractions. Shut off your cell phone. Log off the Internet. Turn off the "dings." Put on a baseball cap and pull down the visor. Single-minded focus. That's where it's at.

THE 80-20 RULE

One day in 1906, an Italian economist named Pareto was working in his garden. As usual, he was lovingly caring for all his plants when he got an idea.

"Wow, every season just a few plants produce the great majority of the good vegetables. I wonder what would happen if I spend most of my energy on just the high-producing plants?"

Pareto started focusing most of his energy on his high-producing plants and the results were startling. With no extra effort, the output from his garden grew dramatically and so was born the 80-20 rule.

80% of your results will come from **20%** of your efforts.

Pareto's observation has been applied to many areas:

Salespeople know that 80% of their revenue comes from 20% of their accounts.

Investors know that 80% of their returns come from 20% of their investments.

And so on.

The key is to figure out which activities are contributing the most to the progression toward your goals. **Here's how to apply the 80-20 rule to your own life:**

Describe one of your goals.

_____

_____

Describe five activities you undertake to help you achieve your goal.

1. _____

2. _____

3. _____

4. _____

5. _____

Which of those activities is moving you closer to your goal most quickly?

_____

Try putting an extra amount of your time into that activity, and see what happens.

33

Effective time management does not mean always being busy.

You see, expending time, in and of itself, is not the route to success. What does lead to success is **effective** time management—using time in a powerful and productive fashion.

Too many people equate being busy with being effective, when in fact one has nothing to do with the other. Keeping busy can be a way for people to convince themselves that they are achieving their goals. But always moving is not the same as moving forward. Busyness is often just tumult—lots of movement and noise without any movement toward your goals.

> "Forget time management. I used to convince myself that I would live by volume ..."
>
> *THE 4-HOUR WORKWEEK*, TIMOTHY FERRISS

Ferriss does not actually mean to forget time management, but forget the idea that being busy is the same as being effective. Reflect on the difference and whether the things that are keeping you busy are actually helping you to achieve your goals.

TECHNIQUES FOR EFFECTIVE TIME USAGE

There are a ton of books on time-management techniques and strategies.

Hey, good news. We have read them all and we are going to summarize them for you.

Pick and choose what you think will work best for you:

1. **Make to-do lists**—no one can remember everything!

2. **Develop a good filing system**—put everything on a particular subject in one place.

3. **Touch just once**—when something comes into your day, whether it's paper or digital, make an immediate decision what to do with it. Don't push it aside to deal with "later" if at all possible.

4. **Learn to discard**—get rid of stuff as soon as you can.

5. **Establish defined times to check e-mails, texts, and phone messages.** Every time you are interrupted from what you are doing, it takes time (after the interruption) to get back into it. Your momentum is broken.

6. **Wear a watch all the time.**

7. **Take action**—when you have something to do that can be accomplished in less than two minutes, do it right away.

8. **De-clutter your workspace.** Excess clutter leads to confusion, which leads to gridlock.

9. **Find 30 minutes of quiet time every week** to reflect on your goals and whether your choices about how to allocate your time are moving you forward at the pace you hope for.

10. **Don't stress**—there is no one way to juggle all the balls. Do the best you can. Don't waste energy and focus on worrying. Do the best you can every day and get a good night's sleep. Then repeat.

4 INTELLIGENCE

Isaac Asimov, the science fiction writer known for his high I.Q., explained that though he is thought of as highly intelligent,

> "those scores simply mean that I am very good at answering the type of academic questions that are considered worthy of answers by people who make up the intelligence tests—people with intellectual bents similar to mine."

He realized that if a mechanic, a carpenter, or a farmer made up the tests, he would score very badly because he could not use his academic training or verbal talents.

There are many different kinds of smart. Successful students recognize and use their particular types of intelligence. They also work to strengthen the kinds of intelligence they need to achieve their goals.

LEARNING STYLES

Everyone learns in his or her own way. You might remember times you've said, "I can't learn from teachers like that" or "I hate lectures." You were talking about your learning style. There are different categories of learning styles—the basic groupings are visual, auditory/aural, read-write, tactile, and kinestetic.

The **visual** learner learns best through aids such as charts, films, pictures, and highlighting with colored markers. A visual learner should try to see things in his or her head.

An **auditory** learner gets information— you guessed it—most effectively through hearing. This type of learner should use tapes, sit where lectures can be heard clearly, and verbally review information.

The **tactile** learner is the touchy-feely person. He or she might use touch to learn by tracing words and writing information that needs to be remembered.

The **kinesthetic** learner needs to involve the body to learn most effectively. He or she might take a walk while studying notes on flashcards.

The **read-write** learner likes written information. This type of learner has it the easiest in academic settings because they emphasize reading, writing, and research.

You can discover your learning style and more detailed explanations of learning styles by finding the "**Barsch Learning Inventory**" or the VARK Learning Style Inventory on the Internet.

MULTIPLE INTELLIGENCES

Howard Gardner, who developed the theory of Multiple Intelligences, defines intelligence as:

> "...the ability to solve problems, or to create products, that are valued within one or more cultural settings..."

There are several reasons why it is useful to a new college student to consider types of intelligence. One is to recognize and value your own intelligence and that of others you work and learn with; another is to develop skills to work effectively with others who may have different intelligence styles.

The following describes the strengths of Gardner's eight intelligence styles:

 **Verbal-Linguistic** people use language well. They like to write, tell jokes and stories, and communicate well with words.

 **Logical-Mathematical** people use numbers well and see patterns easily. They like technology, puzzles, and brainteasers.

 **Visual-Spatial** people use sight to perceive the visual world accurately. They are often best in the arts or engineering.

 **Bodily-Kinesthetic** people use the body and physical movement well. They like sports and projects that involve physical activity.

 **Musical-Rhythmic** people use a strong sense of recognition of the elements of music. They enjoy musical expression whether through singing, playing an instrument, or listening to music.

 **Interpersonal** people use the ability to understand, appreciate, and be sensitive to other people. They have a lot of friends and are happy in a crowd of people.

 **Intrapersonal** people use the ability to know themselves, examining their own strengths, weaknesses, feelings, and opinions. They like to be alone and are independent.

 Naturalistic people use the ability to see patterns and categories and appreciate the items in the natural world. They like natural settings, but also are adept at organizing and collecting many kinds of items.

Emotional Intelligence involves being aware of and managing your own emotions and those of other people.

Psychologist Daniel Goleman explains that E.Q. is as important as I.Q.—and maybe even more important—in determining success in life. Even better, **although I.Q. is something we are born with and can't really change, we can improve our Emotional Intelligence throughout our lives.**

Think about the successful people you know or have heard about. They weren't necessarily the valedictorians of their high school classes, but often the ones who were confident, optimistic, popular, sensitive to the moods and feelings of others, and able to use that knowledge to control a situation. They had Emotional Intelligence.

Goleman divides **Emotional Intelligence** into two categories:

Personal Competence – Your ability to manage yourself, your emotions, and impulses. With personal competence you are self-aware so that you can understand and build on your strengths, improve your areas of weakness, delay gratification, and persist toward your goals. You can control anger and handle stress, and have the optimism to enhance your motivation.

Social Competence – Your ability to handle relationships with others. With social competence you have empathy, the ability to understand and be sensitive to the emotions of others. You can work in a team, relate to people who are different from you, persuade people, and reduce conflict.

GROAN

"A journey begins with the first step."

Groan—you've heard it a million times, but like so many of those old sayings, it is worth thinking about. Although long-term goals are important, it is hard to stick with a difficult project when you keep focusing on the scope of the task in front of you. Persistence comes with taking the first step, and then the next one, and then the next instead of being daunted by the twenty-six miles it will take to complete the marathon.

If you have a twenty-page paper to write, take comfort in knowing that you cannot write all twenty pages at once. You have to write one page at a time. Even before you start writing, you have to do your preparation, your research. By dividing your task into small pieces, scheduling the time to complete each piece, and not worrying about how much is left to do, you will be able to stick with your task. A twenty-page paper, after you have finished your preparation, is just twenty, one-page papers.

You know that you can write one page. **Start with that.**

5 CRITICAL THINKING

"Education's purpose is to replace an empty mind with an open one."

MALCOLM S. FORBES

Did you ever drive somewhere and then wonder how you arrived, because you had no recollection of the journey? Did you ever agree to do something and then realize, too late, that it wasn't something you really wanted to do? Did you ever wonder what you were thinking—or if you were thinking?

Many of us go through our daily lives on autopilot. We don't use careful thinking and sometimes we suffer for that. Real education requires real thinking. You will be bombarded with all sorts of information, both academic and life-experience. **What will you do with that information? How will that information shape the person you are becoming?**

You need to acquire **critical-thinking skills** to get the most out of your college years.

Critical thinking is purposeful, deliberative reflection that leads us to know what to believe or do, what to accept or reject, and what to expect in the future based on present information. Critical thinking is what leads to problem-solving and making sound determinations about our own behavior.

CRITICAL THINKING: WHY?

One of the reasons you go to college is to **grow** and **change**. You especially want your thinking skills to be more sophisticated than they were when you began your higher education.

With critical-thinking skills you know how to be more deliberate in your thinking so you can **understand** and **evaluate** the information and ideas that come your way. With sharp critical-thinking skills, your opinions and the conclusions you draw will be of a higher quality.

But critical-thinking skills can be used in every subject, and in all areas of your life. Not only should they help you decide what information to believe, they should also help you to decide who to be friends with, and even whether or not to go to a certain party.

Critical-thinking skills will also be assets for a career because being able to think well and solve problems are important for any job.

Truly educated people use critical-thinking skills all the time. It is how they use the information they acquire and the experiences they have had to shape the choices they make.

GOOD NEWS: You can improve your critical-thinking skills. In fact, sharpening your thinking ability is what college is all about.

Use the acronym **ACES** to improve your critical-thinking skills:

Analyze: Read and listen carefully. Look for main ideas, supporting evidence, the differences between facts and opinions. Examine assumptions—those of others and your own. Faulty assumptions are where prejudices and bias come from.

Clarify: Make sure you understand all that data coming at you by restating what you read or what people say to you. Ask specific questions. Think about what you need to know in order to understand a situation or a problem.

Evaluate: Make decisions about the validity of the information you acquire, and whether and how you should use it. Consider the consequences of different actions. Determine the value of what you are learning, hearing, and seeing. Judge the quality of your thinking in every situation, being aware of your own fallibility and biases.

See Relationships: As E.M. Forster said: "Only connect." New information relates to other information. Look for connections between the courses you are taking, and between what you are learning now and what you have learned. Look for similarities in words and ideas, in characters and themes, in your own experiences, thoughts, and feelings. Use that information to predict or anticipate probable outcomes.

FACT OR OPINION

It is a fact that college students benefit from First-Year Experience courses.

Did I fool you? Just because someone tells you something is a fact doesn't make it so. What is a fact?

A **fact** is something that can be proved to be true **or** false.

Can we absolutely prove that every college student benefits from a First-Year Experience course? **No.**

Does that mean the statement is a lie? **No.** It is a stated opinion, presented as a fact. (So maybe it's a little lie!)

An **opinion** cannot be proved to be true or false, but can be supported by **evidence** to show its **validity**.

If the statement were to quote several studies with statistics about the benefits of a First-Year Experience course, you might agree with the opinion. **The more facts you have to back up an opinion, the more likely it is that you will convince others that you are right.** Then again, there may be many studies that show something different from the ones cited. Critical thinkers don't need to see the facts that refute a certain opinion to know that they might exist— they know there are two sides to every story.

6 NOTE-TAKING

Start off your first class of your first semester the way successful students do. **TAKE NOTES**.

Often material in a lecture will not be duplicated anywhere else. If you didn't take notes, you're sunk. Even if the lecture material duplicates the textbook, you will have recorded the parts of the readings the professor thinks are important. What do you think will be on a test?

Because you are starting a new endeavor—college—this is a good time to develop new habits.

1. **As soon as you sit down, take out paper and pen (pencil tends to fade).** Most good students keep some kind of notebook, spiral or loose-leaf, for each class. In addition to the notebook for taking notes, you want to have a place to keep handouts you've been given. Keep all materials for each class together in one place.

2. **Put the date, the topic of the lecture, and the page number at the top of the page.** Knowing where the material came in the course of the semester, and what each class or lectures was about, will help you study for exams.

Listen

Don't think about whether you like the lecturer's looks or styles, or whether you are bored or uninterested in the material. Just focus on the words you are hearing. Sit where you can hear well and won't be distracted. Verbal clues that tell you what to write down include the following:

- **A raised voice** – An indication of emphasis
- **Repetition** – If the instructor says something more than once, write it down!
- **Examples** – Illustrations of points or concepts
- **Definitions** – Lecturer gives meaning of words used
- **Enumerations** – "There are three characteristics you should note …"
- **Direct announcement** – "Pay attention" or "This is an essential point"

Observe

Pay attention to the lecturer's body language. He/she will give nonverbal clues as to what you should write down:

- **Writing information on the board** – Copy it
- **Using a power point** – If it is too long to copy, look for the important points
- **Gestures** – Pointing to the board, pounding on the desk, using the hands for emphasis
- **Mannerisms** – The lecturer may emphasize a particular point by an eyebrow raise, throat-clearing, or glancing at the notes

Predict and Ask Questions

Actively engage in the lecture by trying to guess what is coming next; by asking yourself questions to test your comprehension; and by trying to connect the material with things you already know.

You know what to write down—but how should you **organize** it?

You don't want your notes to be random jottings, but arranged in a way that helps you study. There are many organizational methods and you might decide which to use according to your learning style and your professor's lecture style.

Informal Outline – This organizes the material using headings that show the major topics with indentations underneath each heading that include secondary points. You might want to leave a wide margin on the side to write down further explanations or key words.

The Cornell Method – Developed by Dr. Walter Pauk, this method involves making a wide column on the left side of your paper. In the larger, right-hand section, record the important ideas from the lecture. Use the left-hand section to write down questions you have, or ideas you don't understand that you will use to fill in information and to test yourself when studying.

Clustering – This is the most visual style of note-taking. Write the speaker's first main idea in a circle in the middle of the page. Create small circles clustered around the big circle and attached by arrows for examples or secondary information that connect to the main idea. Create a new cluster for each new main idea.

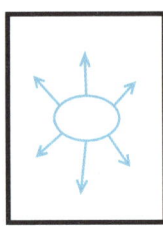

WHAT SHOULD I DO WITH MY IN-CLASS NOTES?

Although writing the information down in your notes is one step toward remembering the material, **it is not enough.**

Successful students:

- **Review notes immediately after a class.** This enables you to fill in extra information, or adjust the organization while the material is still fresh in your mind.

- **Review notes before the next class.** You will be prepared for the next lecture and have a fuller understanding of the material.

- **Review notes when studying for an exam.** You might want to use a study group and compare your notes to others to make sure you have recorded the important information.

There are many established methods of note-taking when you do your reading assignments. They include: *SQ3R, The Cornell Method, Clustering, Note Cards, Triple Underlining, and Summarizing*. It will be easy to find detailed instructions for any of these methods, but they all basically consist of three parts:

previewing, **reading**, and **organizing** the material for study.

PREVIEW + READ + ORGANIZE

Your goal is to create a study guide you can use when you have finished your reading assignment, so you never have to read that chapter again.

Whatever method you choose for organizing your reading, you should work in sections. Do not treat the entire chapter or fifty-page assignment as a whole, but divide it into chunks. Often, a chapter will already be divided by headings. Not only will it be easier to handle your material if it is in shorter sections, it will be easier for you to attack your reading assignment when your task consists of logical pieces that can be assigned allotted study times.

The three stages of the reading process take time. That is why you are expected to spend two to three hours of study time for every hour of class time.

Think of this: The more time you spend creating your **super-duper study guide**, the better it will be. The better your study guide, the better you will do on your exams!

NOTE-TAKING SKILLS FOR READING ASSIGNMENTS

Previewing

Previewing is a thorough perusal of selected parts of the reading selection that involves **asking questions** and **making predictions** before actually reading the material.

Who knew that what you do before you start your reading assignment could be so important? Good previewing helps you focus on the main points of what you are reading, enhances your understanding, and improves your recall.

When you preview, ask questions such as: Is this the topic or the main idea of the selection? What are the key words? Do I know the definitions of the key words? Make predictions such as: this is the author's point of view, this is important information, and these are the main points that will be made. When previewing, analyze the following items:

1. Title

2. Bold Headings

3. Sub-Headings

4. Introductions

5. Summaries or end-of-chapter material

6. Information about the author such as credentials and when the material was written

Some people will tell you to quickly read through a section before making any marks or notations. Others will say you should highlight and/or make notations as you read that first time.

Choose what is **right for you** according to your style, the subject you are studying, and the material you are reading.

Your goals when you do the actual reading are:

Comprehension – Make sure you understand what you are reading. Look up key words that are not defined in the reading, ask yourself questions to see if you can restate the information, and connect what you read with the class lecture or to what you already know.

Selection – Through highlighting and/or explanatory notes in the margin, you are marking the material that will go into your study guide. **Don't mark everything!** Only include the material that is important enough for you to study for an exam. Summarize or restate the points in the margin when you want to consolidate the information or make comments. Do include any points that might have been made by your instructor because you know that he/she considers that material important.

ORGANIZING THE INFORMATION

The last stage of your note-taking process is organizing the information that you have highlighted or noted as you transferred the assigned material into a **study guide**.

The study guide contains only the information you think will be on an exam and that you have made sure you understand.

Once you have created your study guide, you no longer need to use the book for studying.

As always, you can use any format to organize your information. You might even find that a combination of formats works for you. You might create a study guide in outline form, but use 3x5 index cards for important terms you have to memorize. The benefit of index cards is that you can keep them with you and test yourself at random times.

An outline is often the most convenient way to arrange the information in a textbook. When you think about it, textbooks are already arranged in an outline form. They have chapter headings, section headings, and subheadings that can be transferred to your study guide as the headings for your outline.

Remember, do not put any information into your study guide that you don't understand. If a heading is confusing to you, or contains terms you don't know, **put it into your own words** and define the term when you create your **outline** so you are sure to understand everything in your study guide.

TEST-TAKING

Have you ever taken a test **for fun**?

Perhaps you've taken a magazine or online quiz that shows how compatible you and your romantic interest are, or how your fitness level measures up. You take those tests to find out something about yourself. Ultimately, that is what your tests in college are for—they tell you if you:

- have mastered needed information
- can apply what you know to solve problems
- remember critical facts
- can communicate information effectively
- understand the topics in a course
- are ready to move on
- can connect new information to old

WOO HOO!!
I just took a
TEST!

Tests can also be a **wake-up call**: an hour's studying just isn't going to do it;

neither is an occasional appearance in class or sporadic completion of assignments. Tests help clarify and reinforce your knowledge of the subject, so they are learning experiences in themselves.

Tests also tell your instructor a great deal about how well she/he has been teaching the course and if she/he needs to spend more time on certain areas. In addition, of course, they tell the instructor the same things about you that you learned about yourself. Finally, they enable the teacher to have an objective basis on which to give you a grade.

Although we'd like to think that the learning is all that counts, **GRADES MATTER**. They are an assessment of your performance in college that transfer or graduate schools and future employers will look at when they decide whether to accept or hire you. **They become part of your permanent record—that paperwork that will follow you around all your life.** Twenty years from now, when you apply for a job or another degree, a company or a college may still want to see that transcript from college.

You can **improve your test-taking skills**.

There are **three steps** to the process.

1. **Begin preparing** for your tests from the first day of class by attending all classes and taking good notes. If you must miss a class, get the notes from a reliable classmate as soon as possible.

2. **Do all assignments.** Create study guides for the assigned readings. Make a list of things that you don't understand to ask the professor during class.

3. **Find out** what topics and material will be covered on the test.

4. **Combine** class notes, handouts, and study guides from reading assignments into one guide. Create a one-page review sheet to look over before going to sleep the night before, and in the last minutes before your test.

5. **Find out what kind of questions** will be on the test: essay, multiple-choice, short answer?

6. **Make a study schedule** that allocates study times for several days before the test.

7. **Use memory techniques** and allow enough time to memorize terms, formulas, dates, etc.

8. **Go to instructors' office hours,** the tutoring center, or meet with a study group to review and clarify material you don't understand.

9. **Create a pretest** using questions at the end of chapters, questions the professor has asked, and questions you make up. Take your test and allow enough time to correct it and review areas of weakness.

10. **Sleep and eat.** Your brain needs to be rested and fueled in order to function at its best.

TEST-TAKING STEP TWO: TAKING THE TEST

1. **Arrive a little early** so you can choose a good seat (good light, temperature, noise level, away from distractions), relax, and look over your review sheet.

2. **Preview** the exam.

3. **Write down information**, such as formulas or definitions, which you have memorized and might forget during the exam.

4. **Plan your time**, leaving time for review. Spend the most time on questions that are worth the most!

5. **Careful reading** is an essential test-taking skill.

   > Read directions carefully. Note when a question has more than one part. Note where you are to put the T or F in a true/false test. Note if you are directed to answer a certain number of questions rather than all of them.

   > Read questions carefully. Circle key words that tell you what to do, such as "list" or "define." Make sure you answer the question that is asked. Watch for key words such as "why" that asks for a reason, or "what" that asks for an explanation. Pay attention to the words used in the questions. If you don't know the definitions, make your best guess at the meanings using context clues. Think about other questions that have been asked— you may find hints to the current question in other questions.

6. **Answer the easy questions first** but stick to your schedule allowing enough time for all the questions.

7. **Write clearly**. If the instructor can't read what you've written, she or he will probably mark it wrong.

8. **Review the test** when you are finished. Reread the questions. Make sure you've looked at both sides of the paper and haven't skipped anything. Read your answers carefully. **Don't leave early**. (And don't be distracted by students who do leave early—that doesn't mean they'll do well on the test!)

9. **Be willing to change an answer,** but only if you are positive it is wrong. Often the first guess is the right one.

10. **Don't cheat**. You will defeat all the purposes of testing, including the gathering of information about your progress that is valuable for you. Plus, you will eventually get caught! Do you want to think of yourself as a cheater?

1. **Do not look at your grade** and stuff the test into your backpack. A completed test is an extremely valuable learning experience. Pat yourself on the back if you did well. Curse under your breath if you did poorly.

2. **Read the instructor's comments.** They will indicate areas that were troublesome for you. Look at the questions you got wrong. Look for trends.

3. **Analyze your mistakes.** Are there certain types of questions that gave you trouble? Did you not understand some of the material? Were you missing materials because of poor class notes or incomplete study guides? Were wrong answers due to poor reading of directions or questions? Did you make careless errors? Did you prepare well enough? If you did well on the test, analyze that also. What did you do right? You want to be able to duplicate the results on other tests.

4. **Be honest** and sincere about what areas need improvement.

5. **Even though the test is over**, get help on the areas that you do not understand. Much of learning is cumulative. If you haven't mastered one stage before moving on to the next, you will be in real trouble as the semester goes on.

6. **Remember**, a test is an objective assessment of how well you have mastered certain material. It says nothing about your value as a person. Do not let a bad grade get you down. But also remember that you should not be a passive victim. You can get better grades if you actively set about making changes in your test-taking behavior.

7. **Ask** about any opportunity to take a make-up test to raise your grade.

8. **Talk** with your instructor (politely) if you feel that there are mistakes in the grading.

9. **Reward yourself** for good results. You want to reinforce your own good test-taking behaviors.

10. **Save your test.** You may need it as a study guide for the next test, or a midterm or final.

TYPES OF TESTS

Tests can be divided into two types: **recognition** and **recall**.

Recognition tests are the objective kinds of tests: multiple choice, true/false, and matching.

You must recognize the correct answer from the choices given. Find out if points will be deducted for wrong answers; if not, guess and do not leave any questions blank. If it is a true/false test, for instance, you have a **50/50** chance of being right.

Recall tests are the more subjective tests: essays, short answers, and fill-in-the-blanks.

You must supply the information, or recall it from your memory. In the case of essays, and to a lesser extent short answers, you must also use that information, connecting it to other information to create a response. Find out if partial credit will be given for your answers. If so, write as fully and completely as possible about the topic in the hope that you will get something right.

Sherlock Holmes said:

"WHENEVER YOU ELIMINATE THE IMPOSSIBLE, whatever remains, however improbable, **must be the truth**."

He could have been talking about one of the **strategies** for taking multiple-choice tests. There are techniques to help you optimize your results:

- Read the question carefully, **underlining** key words.

- Try to answer **without looking** at the choices. If your answer is among the choices, it is probably correct.

- **Eliminate** the obvious wrong choices to enhance your odds of getting the right answer.

- Read each of the answers carefully, watching for **extreme qualifying words** such as "always" and "never." Those choices are usually wrong. Watch for negatives such as "which of the following is *not*…" Watch for statements such as "all but one," which mean the majority of the options are *correct* except for the right answer.

- Options with **moderate modifying words** such as "often," "most," or "may sometimes be" are often the right answer.

- If two options seem correct, and you have to guess, choose the one that is **longest and most complete**.

- If two options are the same, neither is correct unless there is a choice that **includes both**. For example:
  a. Six
  b. Half-dozen
  c. Both a and b
  d. None of the above

- If two options are **similar**, one is probably correct.

- If two options are **opposite**, one is often right.

- The correct answer should work **grammatically** to complete the sentence started by the question.

- **If you are positive** that two answers are correct, the "all of the above" choice is probably the right one.

TRUE/FALSE QUESTIONS

- **Read every word.** Wrong answers are often the result of missing negatives, or thinking a statement is true when only part of it is true. For a statement to be true, every part of it must be true, while a statement can be false if only a small part is false.

- Watch for those **extreme qualifiers** such as *always*, *only*, or *every*. Statements containing them are usually false.

- Statements containing **moderate qualifiers** such as *often*, *usually*, or *some* are often true.

- Watch for **oversimplification** and **generalizations**. These statements that try to indicate cause and effect or mask complexity are often false.

MATCHING QUESTIONS

- **Read directions carefully**, noting whether you can use items more than once and whether there is the same number of items in both lists.

- **Work from one column.** If you work from the column with the longer entries, it will save time when you read for matches.

- Start with the **matches you know**.

- Apply all **grammar rules** to find the best match.

FILL-IN-THE-BLANK OR SENTENCE COMPLETION QUESTIONS

- Read the question carefully, looking for **key words**.

- Read your answer carefully, making sure it **fits into the sentence** properly.

- Pay attention to the length and number of the blanks. The answer may not be an **exact fit**, but chances are it will be close.

- **Look for clues.** Is there an "an" before the blank? Then the answer begins with a vowel. Does the verb indicate that the answer is singular or plural?

<blank>

61

These questions often strike fear into the hearts of students, but if you follow the steps of **planning**, **writing**, and **revising**, you can handle the challenge.

Treat your test essays as you would any essay: provide a thesis and support and write clearly.

Your goal is to figure out exactly what the question is. It takes some analysis and careful reading. **Ask yourself these three questions:**

1. What task does this question ask me to perform? The clue lies in directive words such as: analyze, compare, define, discuss, summarize, and explain.

2. What is the topic of this question? Look for a word or phrase that tells you exactly what the subject is.

3. What hints does the question give me about my response? Does it ask for certain details to be included? Does it ask for a certain number of reasons to support a claim?

Answering these questions is part of your planning stage. Your thesis will be your answer to the question.

Plan your essay using the brainstorming and outlining techniques for any writing project. Your thesis must be clear and your support specific, using the information you have learned about the topic. Budget your time, making sure you will have a chance to review and revise.

Write using a structure that includes an introduction, supporting evidence, and a conclusion.

Revise checking for clarity, that you have answered all parts of the question, and that your thesis is a genuine response to the essay question.

OVERCOMING TEST ANXIETY

Everyone gets nervous about tests. Some level of anxiety is helpful, making you perform at your best. But too much anxiety can make you feel sick and unable to concentrate.

There are techniques that work to help relieve some of your test anxiety. The more you apply these techniques, the more positively reaffirming testing experiences you'll have!

1. **Cultivate a positive attitude.** Remember, tests are not a measure of your value as a person. You are not doomed to repeat past performances—you do have the power to change.

2. **Prepare thoroughly.** If you feel confident that you have done what you can to succeed, you will be more confident about taking the test. Some of the worst anxiety occurs in students who are unprepared.

3. **Use your instructors** as allies—go for help.

4. **Find study partners** who are not necessarily your friends, but people who will help you do your best.

5. **Sit far away** from other students who might make you nervous. Pay no attention to pretest chatter.

6. **Use relaxation techniques** such as deep breathing, visualizing a good grade, and tightening and releasing muscles.

7. **Divide the questions** and your time into chunks. Applaud yourself when you complete each section.

You will need to memorize material for your tests in college.

Memory is a complicated process that involves short-term, or working memory, and long-term memory. You need to focus on one thing at a time in order to record information into short-term memory.

To transfer information into long-term memory so that you can retrieve it for a test and for further use:

Repeat – Not the most powerful technique, but works better if you try to use the information instead of going over it again and again.

Overlearn – Keep working with the information even after you think you've learned it.

Chunk – Study smaller pieces of information over a longer stretch of time.

Remember the Middle – We tend to pay more attention to beginning and ends.

Feel – Engage your emotions and personalize.

Connect – Connect new information to things you already know.

Create Mnemonics – Use memory tricks such as acronyms.

Use Kinesthetic learning – Mark up tests, write things down, create maps and charts, act things out, make the information funny.

NOTES

8 MIDTERM

You are now **halfway** through your first semester.

This is a great time to turn your critical-thinking skills on yourself. Use your **ACES strategy** (analyze, clarify, evaluate, see relationships) in a purposeful and deliberate way, reflecting on the following areas:

1. Your ACADEMIC PROGRESS
2. Your GOALS and your PROGRESS toward meeting them
3. Your PERSONAL PROGRESS
4. Your FUTURE

You have received your midterm grades by now, or have some other indication of how you are doing. Grades don't evaluate whether you are kind, interesting, funny, or decent—the criteria most of us use in judging others. What they do show is how well you are playing the game of college. To win this game, you have to be purposeful about following the principles of being a successful student:

- BE THERE
- DO THE WORK
- GET HELP
- PLAN
- THINK

If your performance needs improvement, can you trace any problems to a lack of attention to the factors above? Remember, success is largely a matter of persevering in the right way. Perhaps you have had trouble understanding the content of a course, or trouble with a particular instructor's teaching style. Did you go for help or just allow matters to get worse?

Hoping things will get better doesn't make them change. You have to **take action** if you want **better results**.

If your midterm grades are good, congratulations! However, a good performance brings its own perils. In some subjects, the work gets more difficult as the semester goes on. Figure out what you have done that has been so effective, and rededicate yourself to following the principles of success.

Halfway through your first college semester is an excellent time to re-evaluate your goals.

Do you still want what you thought you did? Were you realistic about what you hoped to attain? Do you need to readjust, or even completely **change your direction**?

Perhaps one of your goals was to be on the Dean's List your first year, yet you have discovered that, despite following the principles of being a successful student, you have gotten a C- midterm grade. Perhaps it is more realistic for your goal to be spending a certain number of hours in the tutoring center, or even for you to bring that grade up from a C- to a B- by the end of the semester.

Conversely, perhaps you haven't worked very hard but have attained a B average. Maybe you see the possibility of being on the Dean's List if you work a little harder, and would like to add that to your short-term goals.

Goals should always be re-evaluated. Establish the habit of making midterm one of those times you consider where you are going and how well you are proceeding down the path.

How **YOU** doin'?

Happy?

Depressed?

Disappointed?

Proud?

Are you a little more grown-up than you were a few months ago? How are you handling time management? Have you been behaving wisely in regard to your health, safety, and finances? Are you behaving in accord with your own personal values? Do those values need some readjusting?

How about the new people you've met? Are the relationships you've formed helping or hurting you? Are you allowing yourself to branch out and learn from the many kinds of people you are being exposed to now?

College is not just about academic growth but personal growth as well.

Have you created some beneficial new habits? Stayed away from behaviors that might become bad habits? Thrown out old baggage you don't need anymore? Not too much time has passed, so it should be easy to make changes you see are needed.

Now is the time to start thinking about:

> **Courses For Next Semester.** Re-examining your goals should help you with these decisions. Seek advice from counselors, professors, fellow students, and Web sites. Register as early as you are allowed in order to have your choice of courses and schedules.

> **Next Year's Living Situation.** Residential students need to request dorms or find apartments surprisingly early. Be proactive in creating the best living situation for yourself. Commuting students should also consider their living arrangements. Is it time to leave home? Or should you move back home?

> **Finances.** If you are getting financial aid, make sure your paperwork is in order. Apply for grants. Think about reducing work hours or getting an on-campus job if working has harmed your school performance. Consider a job or volunteer work if you are not spending your free time wisely.

> **Student Activities.** Perhaps you were too overwhelmed at the beginning of the semester to consider the array of clubs, activities, and services available to students. But there are many things going on at college that will help you make friends, enjoy hobbies, further career goals, improve your school performance, improve your health and fitness, or help you give back to the community. Join something!

> **Summer.** Now is the time to check out jobs, internships, and summer school possibilities. If you wait too long, opportunities will be gone.

NOTES

WHAT'S NEXT?
9 MAJORS AND CAREERS

John Lennon said,

> "LIFE IS WHAT HAPPENS TO YOU when you are busy **making other plans."**

And, in some respects, that is true about choosing a career.

Of course you need to start thinking about how you would like to spend your adult years—those 40 years on average between your entry into the workforce until retirement. But, you should **not** feel that the decisions you make today (as a first-year student) are going to bind you to a commitment you may wish to change. Most people hold seven or eight jobs during their working years.

A recent study indicated that only **two percent** of the people surveyed claim to be working in the occupation they had planned when they were eighteen years old. That seems very low—but the point is that you need to remain flexible and open-minded.

Here is our best advice for now:

Start researching careers and opportunities centered on activities you enjoy doing and that you are good at. You probably have some **big-picture ideas** as to the right kind of career for you. Within those categories, start researching the various choices and options you may have upon graduation.

"The reason adults are always asking children what they want to be when they grow up is because they are looking for ideas."

PAULA POUNDSTONE

Most schools encourage you to choose a major at the end of your first year. As we have noted, you should not feel that this choice locks you in. However, at the same time, you do want to start building on your knowledge in a specific area.

The world is moving away from **generalists** (people with a whole variety of disciplines), and toward **specialists** (people with a lot of knowledge about one particular area).

Now is also the time to explore the career development offices at your school. Once you have a sense of the type of activities you would like to build a career, talking to those who have traveled before you can be helpful. Access the experience of advisors at your school who can help you hone in on career options and the kind of curriculum and major that will enhance your development in that area.

FINDING MENTORS

Effective people know that you rarely have to reinvent the wheel.

Whatever you are doing or wish to do, there are people who have already done it. These people are potential mentors.

> A **mentor** is anyone who will give you some of his or her time to guide your passage to the career(s) you are interested in. A mentor might be a graduate student, a teacher, or even someone unrelated to your school who is working in your area(s) of choice.

How do you approach a mentor?

Be straightforward and direct (and polite!). More people will respond positively than you might think.

Find someone who is doing what you want to do.

Ask for ten minutes of their time to give you some personal advice.

Respect their time and don't go beyond what you committed to.

At the end of the ten minutes, ask if they would be willing to receive future questions from you. If so, you have the beginning of a mentoring relationship. If not, ask if they have suggestions of someone who might be open to helping you. **If you don't ask, you will never know!**

Internships can take a variety of forms, but in general they are any situation where you learn by doing (often without pay).

Whether during the school year or during summer break, if you can put yourself in a position to try out your career interest, you are going to realize several benefits:

1. You will gain insight into what the typical day in that career is like.

2. You will begin to meet people who might help you in the future.

3. You may find the activity in that career is not what you hoped for.

There is a great book titled **Flow**, written by Mihaly Csikszentmihalyi. The message of this book is that the happiest people in life are those who are doing what they love to do. The word "**flow**" refers to the state of contentment in activity—when you lose track of time, when you forget to eat, when you don't hear dogs barking.

If you can find the path to a career where you will experience "flow," you will most likely be very successful… **and content**. An internship is one great way to do that.

Of course at some point you will need to get a job. And in that process you will most likely have to give someone your **résumé**, essentially an outline of why you are qualified for the position you desire.

Use these tips for preparing a résumé:

1. **There is a form for résumés that most employers are used to seeing**—your school's career office will likely have forms for you to look at.

2. **Don't get too hung up on one form**, however. There is no one right form.

3. **Highlight points that will be of interest** to a prospective employer. Be careful not to overload the résumé with irrelevant information.

4. **Humanize your résumé**—ultimately the employer wants to hire someone he or she can relate to.

COVER LETTERS

You need to assume that the job you are applying for is very popular and that there are many applicants.

So, you need to create a cover letter that **separates you** from the pack. Something that will grab the prospective employer's attention and cause him or her to read further and look at your résumé.

Here's some advice for writing a powerful cover letter:

1. Don't dally. Your first sentence should say exactly why you are writing.

2. Less is more! Do not overwhelm the reader with too much text. People tend to pull away from lots of reading, even before they get into the substance.

3. Write and then rewrite. Your cover letter will get better with each revision. Oh yes, after your rewrite, do so again.

4. End with a call to action: "I look forward to hearing from you… my e-mail is…" Make it as easy as possible for the reader of your cover letter to contact you.

INTERVIEWS

The interview is probably the **most important** part of the hiring process. Good cover letters and résumés get you in the door, but the interview is where you can shine.

Advice for interviews:

1. **Just be you.** You can't (and don't want to) disguise the true you.

2. **Address the interviewer's questions**—listen carefully to help you discern exactly what he or she wants to know.

3. **Don't be afraid to express how much you want the opportunity.** Don't play coy, and be careful of asking too many questions; you might give the impression that you're weighing other options. Tell the interviewer how much you want the position.

4. **When you sense the interview is over, don't linger.** Don't let the interviewer push you out; leave him or her wanting to spend more time with you.

5. **In closing, ask about the next step.** Ask whether there is more you can provide to help your chances.

10 READING AND WRITING

_____
duh
_____

"I learned how to read and write way back in grammar school," you may be thinking. You did. And those skills have taken you to where you are now, but at this point you're going to have to **step it up!**

The sheer amount of pages you will be assigned to read, and essays, journals, reflection pieces, analyses, discussions, and explanations you will have to write, require that you pay more attention to your skills in reading and writing. Just as you have learned about being more conscious of your thinking by using critical-thinking skills, you should also develop **critical-reading** and **critical-writing** skills.

READING

One of the most useful things you can do right now is find out how long it takes to read a page.

Choose a full page from a textbook and time yourself as you read it carefully. It might take anywhere from two to five minutes, or even longer. Now, when you get that fifty-page reading assignment, you can be more accurate in planning your time.

Before deciding how to address a reading assignment, it is important to consider the **genre** of the reading selection and the **writer's purpose**.

Why is it important to be aware of the genre of what you are reading?

Would you read a comic book the same way you read a current-event article? Would you read a poem the same way that you read a chapter in your Organic Chemistry textbook? Probably, without even realizing it, you have already been employing different skills to read different materials. But you can be a more effective reader if you are conscious of the different skills that you should use.

The broadest distinction in genre is between fiction and nonfiction. People tend to say that nonfiction is true and fiction is untrue, yet many works of literature contain greater truths than an outdated biology textbook. If you think of fiction as works of the imagination, and nonfiction as works based on fact, you are closer to a useful definition. Yet, even then, many essays, memoirs, biographies, and even articles contain so many of the elements of fiction, they are dubbed "creative nonfiction." The skills that are useful for reading fiction should often be applied to these works as well.

Welcome to the world of blurry borders that you will encounter more and more as you engage in **higher-level thinking!**

We want to identify the different genres of writing because different genres are written for different purposes. The writer of a textbook has very different intentions than the writer of a graphic novel. The purpose is the reason the writer wrote the selection. When you consider what result the writer was seeking, you can apply specific reading skills that will help you get the fullest comprehension out of what you read. In addition, applying different reading skills to different types of writing will help you do well when you have to use the material for tests or papers.

There are **three general purposes** that are useful for a reader to consider: *information*, *persuasion*, and *entertainment*.

There is usually overlap in purpose. A writer of an essay may primarily be trying to persuade, but she also may use humor or tell a suspenseful story to entertain her reader and capture his attention. There are those blurry borders again!

INFORMATION

Much of the reading you will do in college is meant to inform. This kind of reading will usually be followed by some kind of test for which you must demonstrate that you have understood the information, and that you can recall the important facts, concepts, and ideas. **When you read for information your goal is to create a study guide to use when you study for your test.**

There are many techniques, such as SQ3R, that have traditionally been taught to help people read for information. All these techniques employ the following basic steps:

Preview (see next page)

If the material is more than a couple of pages, preview and read a section at a time.

Read

This is the step when you actually read all the words in order to comprehend the material and choose the important information to put in your study guide. As you read, look for the answers to questions you posed in the previewing step. Highlight those answers and other important information that you think you need to know for the test. Make notes in the margins or on index cards of concepts, ideas, and definitions that you want to have in your study guide.

Organize the information

Take the important material you selected during your reading and create your study guide using whatever form works for you. You might make an outline, create index cards, make a graphic organizer, or use a combination of techniques. **You can use the headings and subheadings in the chapter to serve as the organizing structure for your study guide.**

Review

Otherwise known as memorizing or studying, this step is when you work with your study guide to enter the information into your long-term memory so it is available for a test or a paper.

Previewing is the careful consideration of a reading selection before you read it.

Often overlooked, this step can increase comprehension and save time when you are actually reading the text. If you have ever tried to organize a stack of papers, you can understand the beauty of previewing. Instead of trying to figure out where everything should go as you weed through your stack, imagine if you had a drawer full of folders that were neatly labeled with every possible category your papers could fit in. You only have to drop the right paper in the right folder as you quickly breeze through your pile. **Think of previewing as making those file folders.**

Begin by reading the title.

Examine every word of that title; look up any of the key words you don't know; ask yourself questions about the title such as "what does the author mean by that phrase?" Make predictions about the title such as whether it might indicate the topic or main idea of the piece, or if it shows the author's opinion of the subject. Write your questions and predictions down so you can focus on them when you read.

After you have thoroughly considered the title, carefully read whichever following items are applicable to your text, continuing to ask questions and make predictions:

1. Introduction
2. Bold headings
3. Subheadings
4. Concluding materials
5. Biographical material about the author
6. Extra information about the selection such as when and where it was written

PERSUASION

Essays are probably the first thing that come to mind when you think of persuasive writing, but there is an element of persuasion in many kinds of writing that might seem objective (newspaper articles), entertaining (novels), or widely accepted as true (works in psychology or philosophy).

Persuasive writing calls upon your best critical-thinking skills because it is trying to mess with your mind. **Before you allow someone's words to cause you to believe, think, or do something, you should evaluate the argument very carefully.**

1. **Identify** whether a selection or a part of a selection is persuasive. Is there a thesis, an opinion, or a selection of information employed to make you think or believe something? Is the author seducing you with words to make you see things the way he or she does?

2. **Find out about the author.** Look for credentials or expertise that would make you give serious consideration to what he or she says.

3. **Withhold your agreement** until you have carefully examined the support of the author's opinions and ideas. What kind of evidence does the author use to prove his or her points? Does it stand up in your court or could you challenge its validity?

4. **Open your mind** to accepting new thoughts and opinions that stand up to your challenges. Being persuaded by worthy ideas is one of the exciting parts of education.

You may doubt the entertainment value of any kind of reading, but even Shakespeare was writing to keep an audience enthralled.

Novels, plays, poetry, and short stories are the kinds of works we think of as meant to be entertaining, but essays, memoirs, and even magazine articles need to keep the reader interested.

It might help to understand writing that is meant to entertain if you expand your definition of entertainment to **enlightenment**.

This kind of writing casts a light on certain truths about life and people without directly telling you what to think. Writing for entertainment appeals to the senses and the emotions to make you feel or know these things, instead of depending on argument. Even the trashiest romance novel or the bloodiest thriller has something to say about love or good and evil.

"TO ENTERTAIN or not to entertain—

That is the question!"

Your job as the reader of entertaining writing is to spot the truths that are presented to you using all or some of the following elements:

 • CHARACTER

 • SETTING

 • TONE

 • FIGURATIVE LANGUAGE

 • POINT OF VIEW

 • THEME / THESIS

 • PLOT, INCLUDING CONFLICT

There is an element of persuasion in writing meant for entertainment. Once you discover what the work is saying, it's up to you to decide whether or not to accept the truth of such observations about life and humanity based on your own emotions, observations, and experiences.

In order to understand what you read you have to be able to **identify** the topics and main ideas of paragraphs and of whole works.

Topic: This is the subject of a paragraph or selection. The question to ask to identify a topic is: Who or what is this about? The answer should come in a word or phrase such as **cell division, depression, the cost of health care, the difference between topic** and **main idea.**

Main Idea: This is what the paragraph or selection says about the topic. The question to ask to identify the main idea is: What point does the author make about the topic? The answer should come in a complete sentence such as **"The difference between topic and main idea is that topic is a subject, expressed in a word or phrase, and main idea is a complete thought, expressed in a sentence."**

TOPIC SENTENCE

Topic Sentence: This term applies **only** to paragraphs.

It is the sentence that expresses the main idea of a paragraph. Topic sentences are the most important and most general sentences in the paragraph, and should relate to all the other sentences in the paragraph.

Not all paragraphs have topic sentences. These handy devices make it very easy for a reader to understand the point of a paragraph. (It's good to use topic sentences in your writing too, to increase your clarity.)

Topic sentences can be found anywhere in the paragraph, but they are often the first sentence. If you begin reading every difficult paragraph by testing if the first sentence contains the main idea, you will find that just searching for the topic sentence aids your comprehension.

WRITING

Almost all students are required to take at least one composition course that ensures they have the basic writing skills to do college-level work. These skills boil down to the ability to write essays and papers that contain a thesis supported by various types of evidence, and that are expressed clearly using proper grammar, syntax, and word choice.

What some students don't take enough notice of (critical thinking) is that all the ingredients of good writing are contained in what they read. It seems like such a simple equation, but it's so true:

The **more** you read, the **better** you will write.

Remember those basic reading terms: topic, main idea, topic sentence? They are the building blocks of your writing.

Writing is a process. Writing anything worth reading (and why would you hand in something that wasn't worth reading?) is a process composed of many steps. Most students would say the hardest part of writing an essay or a paper is beginning. But if you think of your task as working your way through a series of steps, starting your paper is as easy as doing Step 1.

The Writing Process

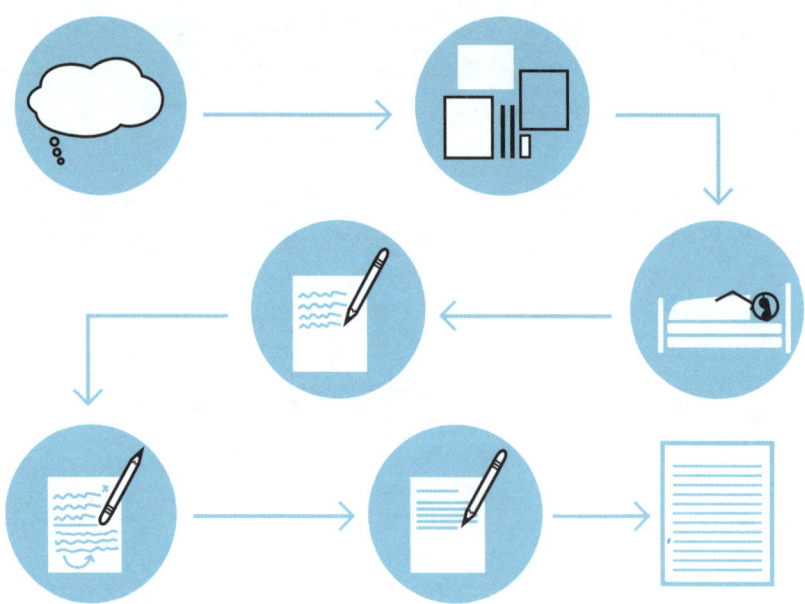

1. PLANNING

2. PREPARING

3. RESTING

4. WRITING THE FIRST DRAFT

5. REVISING

6. EDITING

As with reading, you will probably want to divide a long writing assignment into sections, but be sure to read through your paper from beginning to end when you edit so that you are assured of good continuity.

STEP 1: PLANNING

HINT: GOOD WRITING TAKES TIME.

When students do not plan the time to go through each step of the writing process, the result is an essay or a paper that is poorly researched, poorly written, or does not fulfill the assignment. It's awful to know that you could have done better if you had spent more time.

Completing Step 1 takes care of the time issue while making it easy to begin your assignment. **As soon as you get your assignment:**

- **READ YOUR ASSIGNMENT CAREFULLY.** How long is the paper supposed to be? When is it due? What questions are being asked? Do you have to do research or get materials on reserve at the library?

- **THINK ABOUT THE ASSIGNMENT.** What do you need to do to complete your paper? Can you get a feel for the thesis you will be pursuing, or a direction you want to go in your research?

- **MAKE A SCHEDULE.** Take out your planner and put down exactly when you will go to the library, create an outline, write your first draft, and complete the steps in the writing process. This schedule will make your writing task much easier and ensure that you have enough time to do a good job.

PREPARE.

This step is so easy you don't even have to procrastinate.

The goal of this step is for you to have everything you need when you sit down to write, including materials such as cartridges and paper, or the means and ability to create a PowerPoint presentation. (You may need to find someone to help you.) Your main task in this step is to do your research and take notes so you have all the information you need to complete your assignment.

Take good notes! When you have completed your preparation step, you do not want to have to go back to the sources.

A WORD ABOUT PLAGIARISM: Even with the most honest intentions, it is hard to avoid using the thoughts or words of others. Unless an idea is common knowledge (found in many sources) attribute it to the source.

- **Use your own words when you take notes** so when you write the paper you will already have avoided quoting the source without attribution. If there are phrases that you want to quote, put quotation marks in your notes.

- **Record the citation for each source immediately.** You should have a scrupulous record of every source you have consulted. Find out what type of citation your instructor wants you to use and get the format from your library or online.

RESTING.

You may worry that you are goofing off when you want to take a break or get away from your work. Sometimes you are goofing off, but sometimes you are doing the necessary resting that allows your unconscious to work with the information you have assembled during preparation and make connections. Writing for college may not seem like creative work, but it is, and creative work depends on these interludes when the brain does its work behind the scenes. Most writers find that when they step away from the work they come back with new ideas.

Just don't step away for too long—and be sure to come back!

WRITING.

The moment when you actually have to sit down at the keyboard or paper and write is the hardest. Break this step into smaller pieces.

- **Brainstorm.** Write down your topic and record all your thoughts about that topic as you scan your notes. Write down any main ideas that occur to you. Ask yourself questions to focus your ideas.
- **Organize your ideas.** Make an outline or a map of the information you have jotted down. What ideas go together? What examples or evidence go together? Start molding your outline until you have organized it into a thesis with supporting points.
- **Free write.** Write whatever comes to mind, based on the thoughts and ideas you have organized. Do not listen to your self-censor at this stage—just let it flow.
- **Apply critical reading skills to your free write.** Read over what you have written and look for a sound thesis and evidence that you can develop as support.
- **Create a working thesis statement.** This is the main idea, or the point you will make about the topic. The thesis will guide you in writing your essay or paper.
- **Write your first draft. Don't think of this as a rough draft.** Most likely, your final product will be a revision of this draft. It should be as good as you can make it from the beginning. Your free write was for spontaneous expression; be more deliberate about the first draft. **Hint:** *Try to use topic sentences so you know that each paragraph makes a point that is relevant.*

You do not have to write an entire essay or paper in one sitting. You can divide this step into chunks, handling one section at a time. For instance, you might give yourself an hour to write the introduction in the morning, and two hours to write the body in the afternoon. Remember— schedule enough time to write well.

REVISING.

There is a difference between editing and revising. Revising is not tweaking, it's **surgery**.

This is the stage when you make major additions and deletions. You may move sections around or completely rephrase sentences that are not clear.
Your goal in revision is to make sure that there is a clear point in each paragraph, and that each paragraph contributes to the main points of your writing. You should have no confusion about the thesis or main points, and neither should your reader.

1. **Reread the assignment.** Make sure you know exactly what questions your writing is supposed to answer and what information should be included.

2. **Print your work.** Reading hard copy is very different from reading off the screen.

3. **Read it out loud.** Yes, you will feel like an idiot until you spot those sentences that make no sense when you hear them.

4. **Look for thesis or main ideas, and evidence.** Do you make and support your points? Are your points clear? Is your evidence specific? Do you have ideas that do not contribute, that distract, or that actually damage what you are trying to say? Be ruthless—delete. Do you need more or better support?

5. **Look for clarity.** Should you rearrange the order of what you have presented? Does each sentence make a clear point that a reader (who is not inside your head) will understand? Is your grammar correct or are there run-on sentences and disagreement between subject and verb that will muddy a reader's comprehension of your writing?

NOTE: If your instructor has read a draft and made comments, be sure to incorporate those comments at this stage.

EDITING.

You are almost there. Your major pieces are in place on your paper or essay.

This stage is where you make it pretty.

- Read through your work from **beginning to end**.

- Look for further **grammatical errors** such as verb tense problems.

- Look for **misspelled words**. You cannot only rely on spell-check—it will not fix the mistake if you have confused "there" and "their."

- Check **punctuation**. Are quotation marks used correctly?

- Check for **typos** and **other errors** such as skipped numbers in a list.

- Check **form** and **accuracy** in footnotes and citations.

- Check that the **format** is as required in such areas as the cover page or page numbering.

Put the paper in your book bag and **celebrate** the completion of a good piece of work.

11 SPEAKING

There is nothing more **compelling** than a well-stated oral presentation.

Written words are nice but nothing has an impact over others like the spoken word. And why not? It is how we learned to communicate. And we learned to speak well before we learned to read.

One element of your growth as a college student should be the development of oral presentation skills. And here is something very important to know: **Most great speakers are not naturals.** They were not born with an ability to hold an audience's attention.

Rather, they worked at their skills. They realized the importance of public speaking and made a conscious effort to develop their talents.

"All the great speakers were bad speakers first."

RALPH WALDO EMERSON

TIPS FOR EFFECTIVE SPEAKING

Below are five tips to make your oral presentations as effective as possible:

1. **Less is more.** You know how short your attention span is, so assume that your listeners' attention span is even shorter. Leave your audience wanting more. When you err on length, err on the side of too short.

2. **Interlace your comments with personal experiences.** People love stories. Don't be afraid of appearing stupid in your narratives. We all appreciate people who can laugh at themselves. We all do dumb stuff.

3. **Try to speak without notes for the first and last minutes of your presentation.** You don't need to memorize your comments verbatim. But, it would be nice if you could speak from the cuff at least in your opening and closing.

4. **Speak slowly and look at people.** Scan the audience. Connect with your listener as much as you can.

5. **Try to end with a high point.** What thought do you want to leave your listener with?

Public speaking is an acquired skill. Learning just a few tricks and tips can make you much more **effective**.

SO THIS **ONE** TIME....

Many people are frightened of public speaking. In fact, it ranks right up there with the fear of snakes and heights.

No one in the audience is going to bite you. And it is highly unlikely that you will fall off the stage and hurt yourself. **So, what is the fear about?**

It is about embarrassment. It is about looking silly. Okay, that's understandable, but the fact is that we all do dumb stuff. We all look silly at times. So what? People understand and relate to those who screw up. In fact, making mistakes can be really endearing.

So, just prepare as well as you can (more on that to follow), walk out there and do your best. **You just might surprise yourself!**

PRACTICE, PRACTICE, PRACTICE

There is no better way to enhance your performance and get over any jitters than to **practice, practice, practice** before you ever start speaking a word in public.

Every great speaker **practices** before he or she takes the stage. The idea that people are natural **"ad-libbers"** is a myth.

There are several reasons why practice makes perfect when it comes to public speaking:

1. The more you practice, the more you hone your comments. The content of your speech will improve with each run-through.

2. The more you practice, the more comfortable you will be on "game day." After you have rehearsed your comments (in front of a mirror is good), you become more at ease with the delivery.

3. The more you practice, the more able you are to think on your feet. This one may seem counterintuitive, but the fact is, the more you prepare (practice), the more able you are to vary from the script—you are comfortable when you take the stage and your creative juices can flow.

As with any skill, the more you do it, the better you get at it. The same is true for public speaking. If one of the greatest orators of all time, Demosthenes, can rehearse with pebbles in his mouth (or so the stories go) so he was able to enunciate more clearly when he gave a speech, then certainly the rest of us can practice a bit, too.

THREE THICK THISTLE STICKS
three thick thistle sticks
three thick thistle sticks

12 THINKING GLOBALLY

Perhaps you have heard the expression, **"the world is flat."**

That is also the name of a book written by Thomas Friedman in 2005.

Friedman writes that technology is making it so easy for people all over the world to communicate and compete that no young adult can afford to think parochially ever again. Here is a snippet from Friedman's 500-page book:

> "Globalization 3.0 (today) is shrinking the world from a size small to a size tiny and flattening the playing field at the same time. ... The dynamic force in Globalization 3.0 ... is the new found power for individuals to collaborate and compete globally...
>
> Individuals must, and can, now ask, Where do I fit into the global competition and opportunities of the day, and how can I, on my own, collaborate with others globally?"

The point is actually quite simple.

If you want to succeed in your endeavor of choice you **MUST**:

(1) understand that you may be competing with people halfway around the world;

(2) understand how people of all ethnicities, cultures, and races think and communicate and;

(3) embrace diversity—learn from and grow with those who are not at all like you.

STEREOTYPES

A stereotype is a broad-strokes label put on people of certain races, cultures, religions, sexual orientations, or ethnicities. Stereotypes are impediments to communication and collaboration.

By now you know that everyone is different. This holds true for people of the same race, culture, and ethnicity. As soon as you try to typecast (stereotype) someone, you put a box around both you and them. You see the other people in a way that is most likely not accurate. And, you create a box around yourself because you create distrust and animosity in the other person.

If you are going to see in this FLAT WORLD of ours, you better kick stereotyping this minute. No two people are alike.

You must **embrace** the **differences** in people, the **diversity** in your school, your environment.

We don't learn by surrounding ourselves with people just like us.

Rather, we grow and evolve when we experience new people, places, and things. That is what diversity is all about.

Every single person you meet can help you. Maybe not right now but someday. They can teach you. How you see and experience the world is often very different from how others do. By embracing people of different races, cultures, and ethnicities; of different sexes, sexual orientations, and ages; of different physical and mental talents (and/or disabilities), you learn. **You learn a lot!**

One of the biggest mistakes people make is that they confuse the familiar with the universal. In other words, they presume that what is familiar—i.e., what is comfortable to them—is what is comfortable to lots of others (the universal). In making that mistake they often make significant errors of judgment, miss opportunities, and lose friendships.

GETTING INVOLVED

One great way to enrich yourself is to get involved in community activities— especially with people **NOT LIKE YOU**.

Have you ever worked in a soup kitchen? Do you presume that the people who eat there are very different from you? Maybe they are, maybe they're not. But, in any event, you can learn a lot from people who have been knocked around by life.

There are innumerable opportunities to learn from people different from you. Here are four suggestions:

> Volunteer to work in a drug or alcohol dependency clinic.
>
> Mentor a young adult of a different race than yours.
>
> Work on a political campaign for a candidate you feel strongly about.
>
> Give your time to a homeless shelter, a hospital, or other community organization.

In any of the above environments, you will encounter people experiencing life in a way that may be very different from what you are familiar with. **That is what growth is all about.**

FINANCIAL LITERACY

13

Wow, now we are getting into some **big topics**!

Money is one of those subjects that is very personal. How much do you have? How much do you make? How much do you want? Everyone will answer these questions differently in part because **money involves choices**.

What you make, what you spend, what you save, what you need—in each case the response to these questions will depend upon decisions you make during your life. Some people want as much money as they can possibly make and are prepared to sacrifice other aspects of their life to maximize their income. Other people do not want to center their lives on the acquisition of material items.

One author, T. Harv Eker (Secrets of the Millionaire Mind), speaks to your "financial blueprint: the information or 'programming' (about money) you received in the past and especially as a young child."

There is no right answer of course. **What matters is what matters to you.** For now, however, understand that money is a scarce commodity. That means it goes to those who provide economic value. In order to make a lot of money, you will need to prepare yourself to bring economic value to the business world. We will talk more about this.

In order to achieve the level of financial well-being you desire, you need to understand some basics of finance. There are, of course, a million things to learn. But let's start with five very basic principles:

1. It's not what you make that counts, it's what is left over after you spend what you make. It is your **net income** (after expenses and taxes) that we need to focus on.

2. If you do not track your income and expenses (and taxes), you will never get on top of your financial needs. You must make a **budget**—even if it's something rudimentary.

3. The government wants a portion of what you make. Get prepared to pay **lots** of income taxes over the course of your lifetime.

4. The government also wants you to contribute to your future financial well-being and health-care needs—in the form of **Social Security** and **Medicare**. Deductions for these amounts will come out of your paycheck.

5. **Debt** is the number-one way people get into a serious financial hole from which they cannot extract themselves. You need to be savvy about what you borrow and under what conditions.

There are two purposes to a bank:

1. To help you save, invest, and administer your money—savings and checking accounts, Certificates of Deposit, debit cards.

2. To lend you money—car and home loans, credit cards.

Understanding your options when you walk into a bank is **critical**.

It is also important to understand that bankers are not your friend like your doctor or teacher. Bankers want to make money for their bank. And they want you to help them. So you need to realize that when you invest money in a bank product (e.g., a savings account), you are making the bank money. Ditto when you borrow money from a bank or use one of its loan products such as a credit card. **That is OK so long as the advantages to you of having or using that product are worth the costs.**

"A bank is a place where they lend you an umbrella in fair weather and ask for it back when it begins to rain!"

ROBERT FROST

BALANCING A CHECKBOOK

Balancing a checkbook is a basic component of budgeting.

The old joke,

I CAN'T BE OUT OF MONEY, I **still** have checks in my checkbook

is … well, not funny.

Far too many people never get around to balancing their checkbook—essentially just keeping track of what they have in the account and what is going out with each check—and as a result get hit with lots of fees by their banker.

To balance your checkbook:

1. **Write down in your ledger every check you write and immediately total what you have left after that check.**

2. **Check your ledger against the monthly statement you receive from the bank.**

If you do not balance your checkbook, you are likely to get hit at some point with **"overdraft" fees**. These are fees banks charge you for writing checks that exceed the amount in your checkbook. **They are very expensive!** Wouldn't you rather spend time keeping your checkbook in balance than pay these fees?

CREDIT AND DEBIT CARDS

A **debit card** allows you to access the money in your checking or savings accounts. Most debit cards have ATM capabilities so you can get cash when you need it. A debit card is safer than a credit card in that it is not a vehicle for borrowing money. If you try to use your debit card to purchase an item for more money than you have in your account(s), the purchase may get honored (with an overdraft fee) but at some point your banker will no longer honor these charges.

A **credit card** allows you to borrow money—to buy things with money you don't have. Every credit card has a credit line. For example, if you have a credit line of $500, you can borrow this amount from the bank just by using your card. If you exceed that amount there are fees. Then in a few weeks you will get a bill with a total of all that you owe the bank for the preceding weeks' charges. If you cannot pay the total, you will be charged interest on what you cannot pay. Interest rates on credit cards are quite high—the average rate today is about 15%.

"It is no accident that a credit card is so small and thin and easy to get out of your pocket or purse. If the credit card companies could oil the cards so that they slip out that much quicker, they would do that as well."

JIM RANDEL,
THE SKINNY ON CREDIT CARDS

BORROWING MONEY

Unfortunately, Shakespeare's advice does not work in the 21st century. At some point in your life, and probably sooner rather than later, you will be borrowing money (maybe even lending money). Perhaps you will have and use a credit card. Or, get a student loan ... or a car loan. Or borrow money from your family.

> "Neither a borrower nor a lender be;
> For loan oft loses both itself and friend.
> And borrowing dulls the edge of husbandry."
>
> WILLIAM SHAKESPEARE'S HAMLET
>
> (Polonius giving advice to his son Laertes as Laertes heads off to school.)

The fact is that borrowing money can be of great use to you if you do so **reasonably** and **responsibly**.

Borrowing allows you to purchase items before you have the ability to pay for them in full:

A college education, a car, necessities that you use your credit card to buy.

So long as you borrow with your eyes wide open **(don't kid yourself about your ability to repay the loan)** and with clarity as to the terms and conditions of repayment, then Shakespeare's warning should not apply to you.

UNDERSTANDING YOUR CREDIT SCORE

If you have ever used a credit card, you most likely have a credit score assigned to you. Here is how this works:

There are three major credit reporting companies:

 Transunion,   Experian,   and   Equifax.

These companies are provided information about you from anyone who lends you money (e.g., banks) or has a financial relationship with you (e.g., landlords). These reporting companies compile this information into your credit report. By law they have to give you a copy of your report once a year. Go to **www.annualcreditreport.com.**

Credit scores range from a low of 300 to a high of 850. Your credit score is like a grade card. The scoring company (the biggest is Fair Isaacs Corporation) looks at your credit report and does some fancy mathematics to give you a score. This credit score presumably predicts how you will behave in the future when it comes to repaying lenders or other accounts with which you have an interest.

Your credit score is actually quite important because it is available to lots of people who will have an impact on your life: lenders, landlords, employers, and insurance companies.

One of your high priorities should be doing your best to keep your credit score up. **First rule:** pay your bills on time.

One of the hardest things to do is **"live within your means."**

In other words, keeping your consumption in line with your ability to pay for it. People get into debt problems when they make purchase decisions that are out of whack with their ability to pay for them. And it can all happen so quietly—little by little. Before you know it, big debt issues arise.

Every decision you make—which apartment to rent … how many people to live with … which cell phone service to use … where to shop for clothing and how much to spend … which purchases are essential and which can be put off for another time—must be made in light of your overall financial ability to earn and pay.

We all get impatient. **We all want what we want … WHEN we want it.** But, the key to staying out of financial trouble, out of serious debt, is to exercise patience and prudence in your purchase decisions. (How is that for some serious alliteration?)

"Patience, prudence and parsimony are the preferred purchasing priorities for people in college."

ANONYMOUS

(because no one would admit to having said this)

Before you consider a student loan, you should review all possible grants and scholarships that may be available to you. These, to be contrasted with loans, do not have to be paid back.

There are two main types of student loans: **government** (subsidized and unsubsidized) and **private** loans.

Private student loans come in many varieties. There is usually more flexibility in structuring a private loan than a subsidized loan. The largest private lender in the United States is a company called Sallie Mae.

Although **subsidized loans** require lots of paperwork and take more time to process, explore these loans in full before considering a private loan (or additional private lending). The interest rates on these loans are usually about half the amount of private loans. There is no requirement to make payments while you are in college. There are flexible repayment terms. There are, however, annual limits to what you can borrow—and a lifetime total as well.

IMPORTANT: Student loans are serious business. If you have financial trouble later in life and ever have to consider bankruptcy (a legal process for wiping out all your debts), one of the few debts that is not wiped out in bankruptcy is a student loan!

INCOME TAXES

Ouch! Sorry, but this subject just **can't be avoided**.

Like it or not, this is a subject about which you need to have a basic understanding.

The United States collects its income taxes in two ways:

1. **Income taxes are withheld from your paycheck by your employer.** This calculation is based on the number of exemptions you claim. When you get hired for a job you will fill out a Form 9, which tells the government how many exemptions you claim. For simplicity, think of an exemption as you and anyone else who is dependent on you for his or her care. The fact that the government withholds money from your pay does not mean you will have to pay that withheld amount in taxes. The withheld moneys often come back to you at the end of the year based on what you actually owe versus what was withheld from your income. The withholding is just to be sure you don't forget to pay your taxes.

2. **Every year U.S. citizens are required to pay by April 15th the taxes they owe the government for the preceding calendar year.** A tax return starts with Gross Income (everything you earned), minus your exemptions and deductions (for most students this is a set amount—what is called the standard deduction) to derive Taxable Income. A tax rate is then applied to your Taxable Income.

"Every year the government shoves you in a river with all your earnings in your pocket, whatever doesn't get wet you can keep."

WILL ROGERS

One of the lessons you can learn from senior citizens is that the decisions you make as a young adult will greatly impact your life in later years. How much you save. Your investment decisions. Debts or no debts.

That is why it is so **critical** that you use your college years to learn all you can about the financial world. You must **educate yourself** about the basics and not blindly take advice from anyone who has an agenda that may not be in your best interest.

Here is our **NUMBER ONE**
rule for financial decisions.

If you do not fully understand a product, offering, or opportunity being proposed to you, **THEN PASS**—do not contribute your hard-earned dollars to something you do not totally comprehend.

Some people are dishonest and will suggest expenditures or investments that are just plain bad. Most people are honest but have to make a living and in doing so, don't always explain as carefully as they should all the plusses and minuses of various financial decisions.

"Use your time in college to boost your street smarts … learn everything you can about banking, income taxes, investments, debt and credit, insurance and career opportunities. The time you spend today—**to make yourself as financially savvy as possible**—will stand you in good stead as you bob and weave through the complicated financial world waiting for you outside your campus walls."

Jim Randel, The Skinny on Finance for the Young Adult

14 HEALTH

There are three types of health:

physical (body), mental (brain), and emotional (spirit).

College is a time of stress. Of too much to do with too little time to do it in. Of finding yourself. Of new experiences—some pleasant, some not. And then just when you start getting comfortable, college ends with a whole slew of new challenges—getting a job, making ends meet, crafting a future for yourself.

One of the most important pieces of advice available to you is that your enjoyment of college life, your ability to deal with competing stresses and pressures, your facility for "rolling with the punches," will be enhanced by the attention you pay to your health—mental, physical, and spiritual.

The pages that follow are about paying attention to **YOU**— making your health a priority and finding a balance between your needs and all that you need to do and be.

THE BASICS OF GOOD NUTRITION

For the most part, the path to good health is quite well marked:

1. Eat the right foods
2. Drink lots of fluids
3. Exercise
4. Get adequate rest

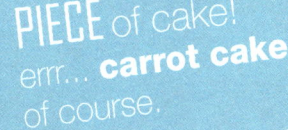

PIECE of cake! err... **carrot cake** of course.

The challenge, of course, is finding the **time** and the **discipline** to do all the right things.

Let's start with nutrition. Here are **eight very important rules** of good nutrition:

1. Eat a good breakfast.

2. Eat five or six times during the day—rather than two or three huge meals.

3. Eat lots of vegetables.

4. Eat lots of fruit.

5. Drink lots of water.

6. Moderate your intake of white flours and sugars.

7. Don't eat right before going to bed.

8. Read labels—know what you are putting in your system.

That's it. If you are conscientious about those eight rules, you are on your way to a healthy body.

"A GOOD LAUGH AND A LONG SLEEP are the **best cures** in the doctor's book."

Irish proverb

"IF WE WERE MEANT TO POP OUT OF BED, we would sleep in **toasters**."

Anonymous

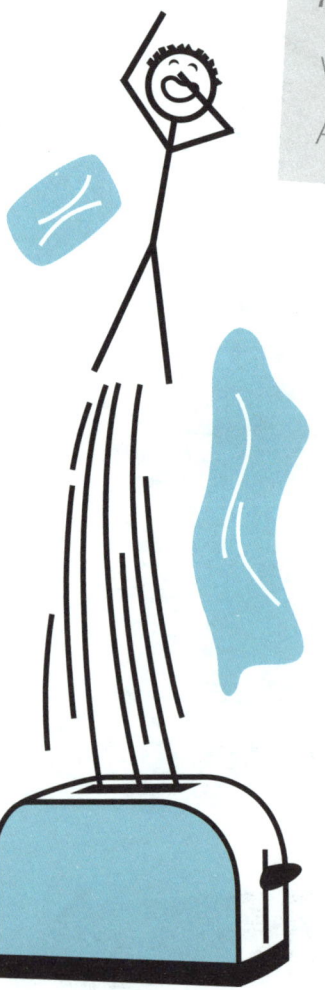

OK, you get it.

Sleep and rest are critical to rejuvenate your system. And for most, college is a time that challenges your need for sleep. Many students report feeling sleep-deprived **50% of the time.**

The fact is you can fool your body for short periods of time and function relatively well on less than six to eight hours of sleep per night. But, eventually your body's need for rest will catch up to you.

Note the "six to eight" hours of sleep. While most experts suggest eight hours, there are some people who function well on an hour or two less. But, anything under six hours a night is not considered healthy.

THE RIGHT EXERCISE PLAN FOR YOU

OK, now for some very exciting information. We have discovered the **Fountain of Youth** and we are going to tell you where it is. It is right outside your door!

Study after study after study have all established the benefits of exercise for longevity and good health. So, let's say you buy into the benefits of exercise. **What is the right plan for you?**

Well, experts would tell you that you should try to do something—anything that causes you to move—for about 30 minutes a day. That does not mean you need to visit the gym every day.

Any activity that causes you to work your body is good.

A brisk walk. A climb up the stairs instead of an elevator. Helping your friend move to a different dorm room. Whatever. **The point is to use that amazing body of yours.**

And for those of you who want to go the next level, physicians suggest four to five days a week of moderate to strenuous aerobic exercise. On some of those days, weight-training is also suggested. Five to six days in the gym should be enough, however. Almost everyone suggests one day off!

If there is a Fountain of Youth, there is also a Well of Abuse. Drugs can be just as devastating to human life as disease, accidents, and wars. Drugs and alcohol usually kill you slowly. The disease creeps up on you.

You know the facts.

You know the statistics on drug and alcohol use. So, if you want to experiment, that is your decision. But, **don't fool yourself. Drugs and alcohol are addictive.**

At least consider this one plea: **EVERYTHING IN MODERATION.** Drug and alcohol use to the extreme can kill you—and in some cases, not slowly. Every year there are stories of young adults who went too far—and who are no longer around to talk about it.

I'M OK, YOU'RE OK

One of the most important lessons a person learns over a lifetime is that there are few "normals." **We are all different.** We all have issues and history and pressures to deal with. And the best we can do—is the best we can do.

"Most people are about as happy as they make up their minds to be."

ABRAHAM LINCOLN

One stress we want to diffuse right now, however, is the worry that you are different from others—and thereby somehow less worthy or valued.

You are you. That's that and now move on. Be the best YOU can be. And then be happy.

HOW TO STICK TO YOUR PLAN

Once you decide on a plan that will enhance your health—whether it is eating better, exercising more, or staying away from drugs/alcohol—the trick (of course) is to **stick to the plan.**

Here are a few suggestions that may help you:

1. **Decide** in advance where you are likely to have problems.

2. **Figure out** exactly what you will do when you are in those challenging situations.

3. **Create** a mantra for yourself when you feel like you are losing the ability to stick with your plan. Repeat your mantra over and over.

4. **Plan** on slipping. We all slip at times. But, you can rebound by planning exactly what you will do after you slip—to get you back on track.

Oftentimes, the way to stick to a plan is to visualize and strategize all the situations where you may fall off your program. By doing that, you create responses that will help you stay the course.

WILL POWER AND SELF-DISCIPLINE

As it happens, Teddy Roosevelt knows a lot about self-discipline. Born very sickly (his mother remarked he looked like a "terrapin"), Teddy struggled with all sorts of illnesses during the first ten years of his life.

One day his father pulled him aside and said, "Teddy, you have the mind but without the body, you will never go as far as you might."

"The one quality which sets one apart from another—the key which lifts one to every aspiration while others are caught up in the mire of mediocrity—is not talent, formal education, nor intellectual brightness; it is self-discipline. With self-discipline, all things are possible. Without it, even the simplest goal can seem like the impossible dream."

TEDDY ROOSEVELT

It is reported that young Teddy said,  "I will make my body." And he created an incredible physical regimen for himself, remaking his body and health along the way.

15 SELF-ASSESSMENT

You've been involved in **assessment** for your whole school life.

Every test you take is an assessment of how well you have mastered certain material. Every report card you got was an assessment of your performance as a student. Yet these are all someone else's assessment of you. Now that you have begun this new educational journey, more and more you need to be engaged in self-assessment.

You've read about critical thinking mostly in terms of all the new information that is coming at you in college. However, one of the most valuable areas on which to focus your critical-thinking skills is **yourself**. Self-awareness is a hallmark of a truly educated and mature person, because it is only when we are aware of who we are, our strengths and weaknesses, our hopes and dreams, the way we are perceived by others, our values and how true we stay to them, that we can make progress as students and as people.

Try this little exercise. ➡ Answer the question, **"Who am I?"**

Write down ten things that you are. Look at that list. Why did you choose the items that you did? Are they the most important things about you? The things that first came to mind? Do you want to make some changes? Go ahead. Now look at each item on your list and write down the things that you like about that quality.

1.

2.

3.

4.

5.

6.

7.

8.

9.

10.

For example, perhaps you wrote "reader" on the list. What you like about being a reader is that you know a lot about people, places, ideas, and history that you would never have discovered in "your own little world." Also, as a reader you have a rich source of entertainment that is easily accessible and keeps you thinking and happily absorbed.

Now that you are **more conscious** of what you like about being a reader, you will make more time for reading. If, however, there was little you could find to like about something on the list, you might try to remove that identity from your list and yourself.

VALUES

Below is a list of twenty values and interests. Rate them from most important **(to you)** to least important.

This reflection is purely for your benefit, so be honest and thoughtful (see ACES, p. 44). Don't rate them the way you think you should, but according to what you **truly believe**.

1. Honesty	**7.** Health	**14.** Learning
2. Friendship	**8.** Safety	**15.** Individualism
3. Family	**9.** Kindness	**16.** Independence
4. Having fun	**10.** Laughter	**17.** Freedom
5. Love	**11.** Money	**18.** Politics
6. Service to others	**12.** Religion	**19.** Relaxation
	13. Work	**20.** Possessions

Did you have some difficult decisions? Were you surprised at some of the choices you made? A self-aware person is conscious of the values that underlie his or her actions.

Your values have an impact on everything you are and do. Your assessment of your goals, the way you spend your time, and the way you spend your money need to reflect the values you hold dear.

MISSION STATEMENT

Goals tell you where you want to go, but your **mission statement tells you where you want to end up**. Writing a mission statement gives you an opportunity to think about what you want your one and only life to mean now, when the choices you make will have such a huge impact on the person you will become.

Answers to these questions will help you create a **mission statement**:

- What do I want people to say about me when I'm gone?
- What makes me feel good about myself?
- What or who inspires me the most?
- What causes do I believe in or care about?
- If I could make a statement that would go out to the world, what would I say?

Your mission statement can be a series of statements such as:

I will contribute to society by giving time and money to charity organizations.

I will make use of my talents and abilities to create a good life for myself.

I will work hard and play hard.

Or your mission statement can say,

My mission in life is:

To be honest at all times.

To take care of my family.

To work hard to meet the challenges I encounter every day.

However you put it, just painting the big picture of what you want your life to mean should make clear to you what is most important to you.

Life provides a series of choices. You should be conscious of the **values**, **beliefs**, and **ideas** that guide the choices you make.

Self-assessment involves an honest appraisal of outcomes. This appraisal includes investigation into the reasons you got the results that you did.

Who is **in control** of your life? Hopefully your answer is **"I am."**

Let's test how much you actually believe that:

Are most things that happen to you the result of **your thoughts or actions?**

OR

Are most things that happen to you the result of **circumstances beyond your control?**

It's tempting to take credit for the good things, and to blame others for the bad. But the minute you see power over your life as residing outside of yourself you have become a **victim** rather than a **controller**.

When you see events happening because of actions you did or did not take, you know that you create your own outcomes. It's easy to accept that idea when it comes to getting an A on the test. Clearly, it's because you studied the right things for long enough, and used your best test-taking skills. But what if you did those things and got a bad grade on the test? Not your fault, right? It was your lousy teacher, or the fact that you are just not good at math.

Here is where seeing yourself as the controller makes a difference.

If you view a failing grade as confirmation that you are stupid and therefore shouldn't even try to succeed in the course, or that the teacher is a student-hating know-nothing, you probably will fail the course. Instead, turn your critical-thinking light on.

Analyze what happened, **clarify** your beliefs about causes to test the validity of them, and **evaluate** the possibilities of different ideas. See the relationships between the things you did or did not do, and the final outcome. **Different actions will change an outcome that you don't like.**

In the case of the failed test, what can you do so the next test will give you a different result? The possibilities are vast:

- Go to the tutoring center
- Form a study group
- Speak with the professor during office hours
- Work longer on your assignments so you are more prepared
- Study harder
- Review your test-taking skills

When you see the control over an outcome as residing in you rather than outside of you, **you have power over the outcome** rather than being a victim of circumstances.

When we take responsibility we change our actions, but it also helps to change our attitudes. We all have running sound tracks in our brains. You know, those times when you say to yourself,

"**You idiot,** of course Stephanie said she was busy when you asked if she wanted to study with you after class. She probably knows that you're stupid in math, and who could miss that huge pimple on your chin?"

That sound track is called **Self-Talk**. When self-talk is a constant negative stream (including calling ourselves names), it's almost impossible to improve outcomes that we don't like. When we see things in a new light, we can change our actions and results, or at least change the way we feel about what happens.

Using **positive self-talk**, after Stephanie's rejection, you might think:

"Stephanie is probably telling the truth about being busy. She rushed off—maybe she has another class. How could she know I'm stupid when the one time I answered a question in class I was right? And she's seen me without a pimple, so that one blemish isn't going to turn her off; in fact, I'm not a bad-looking guy. My mother told me so. I'll ask Stephanie if she wants to get together before class next week, maybe she'll have more time."

What's the **optimistic response** if Stephanie says no again?

"She's just one person who doesn't really know me. I'm sure there are other girls who will appreciate me; there have been in the past. I'll just take my time and get to know more people."

Part of self-assessment involves looking at your performance in the most positive way so that you can try again and do better in the future.

Many people, when asked why they don't do their assignments, study for tests, or even exercise on a regular basis, will answer that they are lazy.

What is laziness?

If you played a video game rather than revising your English essay, you were lazy, right? Yet if someone showed you a film of yourself playing your game, would you look like your idea of a lazy person? Or would you look active and involved?

Maybe what we think of as laziness is simply about making choices.

When we choose the fun and easy thing that brings immediate satisfaction, rather than the more boring and difficult thing that won't pay off for a while, that's when we call ourselves lazy.

Some people seem to be able to make the hard choices easily. They do the extra math problems to better understand a challenging concept, instead of going to a party, because they are keenly aware that the pleasure of getting what they want in the long run (a good grade in math so they will be on the Dean's List) will be much greater than the pleasure of going to one party. They have **motivation**, the ability to move toward a desired goal.

When you engage in self-assessment, it is important to look at your level of motivation and determine **what is stopping you** from moving toward your goals.

Just a few obstacles you may face are:

- Your goals are not authentic (truly yours) or realistic

- You have no short-term goals that you can meet relatively quickly to give you an incentive to keep moving

- Your goals are not compelling—you don't want them enough to delay gratification of immediate satisfaction

- You fear failure

- You fear success

- You fear change

Once you have analyzed the obstacles to motivation, you can **make changes** in what you do or think to help you **move toward** the things that you want.

The opposite of movement is stagnation.

Success—we all want it whether it's in school, careers, or relationships.

As your first semester comes to a close, who can tell you whether you have been successful? You know the answer. Some assessments of your success are **tangible**:

- **Grades, honors, and awards**

- **Registration for next summer**

- **Meeting goals**

- **New friendships**

- **Familiarity with the services in your school that will help you**

- **Good relationships with faculty and staff**

- **Involvement with clubs, student activities, or service learning**

- **Healthy lifestyle**

Some of the assessments of your success, however, are more **abstract**. They are the ones that point to your growth as a student, a person, and your ability not only to achieve success, but also sustain it over time:

- **Growth in a critical-thinking ability**

- **Growth in emotional intelligence, especially optimism**

- **Positive self-talk**

- **Goals that are compelling, measurable, and realistic**

- **A clearer understanding of your values and an effort to live by them**

- **A sense of your mission in life**

- **Responsibility**

- **Motivation**

What **grades** do you give yourself on all of the above items?

Find **accomplishments** to celebrate; there are always some.

Analyze your disappointments and **review** what you have learned about ways to get better results.

As long as you are **engaged** in the process of working on your success, you are on your way to **achieving** it.

MON	TUE	WED
1 Ramadan	2	3
8	9	10
15	16	17
22	23	24
29	30	31 Eid al-Fitr
5	6	7

- Pell Grant
- Work-Study
- Stafford Loan

Money
MATTERS

Getting to **college** takes more than your mighty intellectual resources—it also takes the almighty dollar! Fortunately, there are many ways to fund this investment in your future. Get acquainted with the terms above—then do some research to decide if any of these options are right for you!

THURS	FRI	SAT	SUN
4	5	6	7
11	12	13	14
18	19	20	21
25	26	27	28
1	2	3	4
8	9	10	11

SEP T F S S / M T W T F S S / M T W T F S S / M T W T F S S / M T W T F
1 2 3 4 / 5 6 7 8 9 10 11 / 12 13 14 15 16 17 18 / 19 20 21 22 23 24 25 / 26 27 28 29 30

AUGUST

AUG M T W T F S S / M T W T F S S / M T W T F S S / M T W T F S S / M T W
1 2 3 4 5 6 7 / 8 9 10 11 12 13 14 / 15 16 17 18 19 20 21 / 22 23 24 25 26 27 28 / 29 30 31

GOALS **FTW**

Ramadan

MON

1

TUE

2

WED

3

TODAY'S **DO OR DUE:**

Scholarship **RESOURCES**

Looking for **scholarships?** Check out your school's financial aid office or your academic department. There are also hundreds of resources online. Here are a few good places to start:

• www.studentaid.ed.gov • www.students.gov • www.collegeboard.com

SEP T F S S / M T W T F S S / M T W T F S S / M T W T F S S / M T W T F
1 2 3 4 / 5 6 7 8 9 10 11 / 12 13 14 15 16 17 18 / 19 20 21 22 23 24 25 / 26 27 28 29 30

2011

TODAY'S **DO OR DUE:**

THUR

4

FRI

5

SAT

6

SUN

7

LOOKING BACK

Check IT!

✓ I totally **aced it**
→ still in **progress**

AUGUST

AUG | M T W T F S S / M T W T F S S / M T W T F S S / M T W T F S S / M T W
| 1 2 3 4 5 6 7 / 8 9 10 11 12 13 14 / 15 16 17 18 19 20 21 / 22 23 24 25 26 27 28 / 29 30 31

GOALS FTW

MON

8

TUE

9

WED

10

TODAY'S DO OR DUE:

LOANS: What's the Difference?

Understanding the **different types of loans** can save you major moolah after you graduate. Federal loans have a fixed interest rate of 6.8%. Interest rates on private loans are not fixed and often in the neighborhood of 15%—before fees. In this way, using a private loan is much like paying your tuition with a credit card!

SEP T F S S / M T W T F S S / M T W T F S S / M T W T F S S / M T W T F
1 2 3 4 / 5 6 7 8 9 10 11 / 12 13 14 15 16 17 18 / 19 20 21 22 23 24 25 / 26 27 28 29 30

2011

TODAY'S **DO OR DUE:**

THUR

11

FRI

12

SAT

13

SUN

14

LOOKING BACK

Check IT!

✓ I totally **aced it**
→ still in **progress**

AUGUST

AUG M T W T F S S / M T W T F S S / M T W T F S S / M T W T F S S / M T W
1 2 3 4 5 6 7 / 8 9 10 11 12 13 14 / 15 16 17 18 19 20 21 / 22 23 24 25 26 27 28 / 29 30 31

GOALS FTW

MON

15

TUE

16

WED

17

TODAY'S DO OR DUE:

Fast Facts: SCHOOL STATS!

(Source: National Center for Education Statistics)

- The average tuition rate for public colleges rose by 30% between the '97-'98 and '07-'08 school years (adjusted for inflation).

- In the '07-'08 school year, 66% of undergraduates received financial aid, at an average of $9,100 per student.

- In 2006, the average difference in yearly pay between high school graduates and college graduates was $20,000 for males and $17,000 for females.

SEP   T F S S / M T W T F S S / M T W T F S S / M T W T F S S / M T W T F
        1 2 3 4 / 5 6 7 8 9 10 11 / 12 13 14 15 16 17 18 / 19 20 21 22 23 24 25 / 26 27 28 29 30

2011

TODAY'S **DO OR DUE:**

THUR

18

FRI

19

SAT

20

SUN

21

LOOKING BACK

Check IT!

✓ I totally **aced it**
→ still in **progress**

AUGUST

AUG M T W T F S S / M T W T F S S / M T W T F S S / M T W T F S S / M T W
1 2 3 4 5 6 7 / 8 9 10 11 12 13 14 / 15 16 17 18 19 20 21 / 22 23 24 25 26 27 28 / 29 30 31

GOALS **FTW**

TODAY'S **DO OR DUE:**

MON
22

TUE
23

WED
24

Read ON!

Still feeling **overwhelmed**? Take some advice from the experts!
Check for these titles at your school library:

Zero Debt for College Grads – Lynnette Khalfani
Broke!: A College Student's Guide to Getting By on Less – Kaplan
The Money Book for the Young, Fabulous, & Broke – Suze Orman
Paying for College Without Going Broke – Princeton Review

SEP T F S S / M T W T F S S / M T W T F S S / M T W T F S S / M T W T F
1 2 3 4 / 5 6 7 8 9 10 11 / 12 13 14 15 16 17 18 / 19 20 21 22 23 24 25 / 26 27 28 29 30

2011

TODAY'S **DO OR DUE:**

THUR

25

FRI

26

SAT

27

SUN

28

LOOKING BACK

Check IT!

✓ I totally **aced it**
→ still in **progress**

29	30	31 Eid al-Fitr
5 Labor Day	6	7
12	13	14
19	20	21
26	27	28
3	4	5

GOAL-
Setting

The future is full of **possibilities**—where do you want it to take you? Setting personal goals is the best way to achieve your dreams! A good goal is set by figuring out what you want, how you can do it best, and when you want to achieve it.

THURS	FRI	SAT	SUN
1	2	3	4
8	9	10	11 Patriot Day
15	16	17	18
22	23	24	25
29 Rosh Hashanah	30	1	2
6	7	8 Yom Kippur	9

OCT   S S / M T W T F S S / M T W T F S S / M T W T F S S / M T W T F S S / M
1 2 / 3 4 5 6 7 8 9 / 10 11 12 13 14 15 16 / 17 18 19 20 21 22 23 / 24 25 26 27 28 29 30 / 31

SEPTEMBER

SEP
T F S S / M T W T F S S / M T W T F S S / M T W T F S S / M T W T F
1 2 3 4 / 5 6 7 8 9 10 11 / 12 13 14 15 16 17 18 / 19 20 21 22 23 24 25 / 26 27 28 29 30

GOALS **FTW**

TODAY'S **DO OR DUE:**

MON

29

AUG

TUE

30

AUG

Eid al-Fitr

WED

31

AUG

Goal-Setting **RESOURCES**

Goal-setting is **crucial** in order to get the most out of your college experience. There are also online resources to help you take charge of your future. Here are a few places to start:

• www.goal-setting-resources.com/
• www.stephencovey.com
• www.collegegoals.com/resources/online_resources.html

OCT S S / M T W T F S S / M T W T F S S / M T W T F S S / M T W T F S S / M
1 2 / 3 4 5 6 7 8 9 / 10 11 12 13 14 15 16 / 17 18 19 20 21 22 23 / 24 25 26 27 28 29 30 / 31

2011

TODAY'S **DO OR DUE:**

THUR

1

FRI

2

SAT

3

SUN

4

LOOKING BACK

Check IT!

✓ I totally **aced it**
→ still in **progress**

SEPTEMBER

SEP | T F S S / M T W T F S S / M T W T F S S / M T W T F S S / M T W T F
1 2 3 4 / 5 6 7 8 9 10 11 / 12 13 14 15 16 17 18 / 19 20 21 22 23 24 25 / 26 27 28 29 30

GOALS FTW

Labor Day

TODAY'S **DO OR DUE:**

MON

5

TUE

6

WED

7

SHORT-TERM GOALS: A stepping stone for success

Short-term goals are the **baby steps** to reach the big-picture goal at hand. Start by identifying a goal for the current semester and any potential stumbling blocks. What will you do to prevent or overcome them? Be sure to identify the rewards for completing your short-term goals!

(Source: www.brookhavencollege.edu/studentsvcs/counseling/goal-setting.aspx)

OCT   S S / M T W T F S S / M T W T F S S / M T W T F S S / M T W T F S S / M
     1 2 / 3 4 5 6 7 8 9 / 10 11 12 13 14 15 16 / 17 18 19 20 21 22 23 / 24 25 26 27 28 29 30 / 31

2011

TODAY'S **DO OR DUE:**

THUR

8

FRI

9

SAT

10

Patriot Day

SUN

11

LOOKING BACK

Check IT!

✓ I totally **aced it**
→ still in **progress**

SEPTEMBER

SEP | T F S S / M T W T F S S / M T W T F S S / M T W T F S S / M T W T F
1 2 3 4 / 5 6 7 8 9 10 11 / 12 13 14 15 16 17 18 / 19 20 21 22 23 24 25 / 26 27 28 29 30

GOALS **FTW**

TODAY'S **DO OR DUE:**

MON

12

TUE

13

WED

14

OCT | S S / M T W T F S S / M T W T F S S / M T W T F S S / M T W T F S S / M
1 2 / 3 4 5 6 7 8 9 / 10 11 12 13 14 15 16 / 17 18 19 20 21 22 23 / 24 25 26 27 28 29 30 / 31

2011

TODAY'S **DO OR DUE:**

THUR

15

FRI

16

SAT

17

SUN

18

LOOKING BACK

Check IT!

✓ I totally **aced it**
→ still in **progress**

SEPTEMBER

SEP T F S S / M T W T F S S / M T W T F S S / M T W T F S S / M T W T F
1 2 3 4 / 5 6 7 8 9 10 11 / 12 13 14 15 16 17 18 / 19 20 21 22 23 24 25 / 26 27 28 29 30

GOALS FTW

TODAY'S DO OR DUE:

MON

19

TUE

20

WED

21

Read ON!

Looking for ways to **ensure** your goals **stick**?
Check out these titles from your school library:

- *The Ten Commandments of Goal Setting* – Gary Ryan Blair
- *What Do You Really Want?* – Beverly K. Bachel
- *Write it Down, Make it Happen: Knowing What You Want and Getting it* – Henriette Anne Klauser

OCT
S S / M T W T F S S / M T W T F S S / M T W T F S S / M T W T F S S / M
1 2 / 3 4 5 6 7 8 9 / 10 11 12 13 14 15 16 / 17 18 19 20 21 22 23 / 24 25 26 27 28 29 30 / 31

2011

TODAY'S **DO OR DUE:**

THUR

22

FRI

23

SAT

24

SUN

25

LOOKING BACK

Check IT!

✓ I totally **aced it**

→ still in **progress**

SEPTEMBER

SEP T F S S / M T W T F S S / M T W T F S S / M T W T F S S / M T W T F
1 2 3 4 / 5 6 7 8 9 10 11 / 12 13 14 15 16 17 18 / 19 20 21 22 23 24 25 / 26 27 28 29 30

GOALS FTW

TODAY'S DO OR DUE:

MON

26

TUE

27

WED

28

Quote THIS!

"If you don't know what you want, you will probably never get it."

OLIVER WENDELL HOLMES SR.
American writer and physician

OCT S S / M T W T F S S / M T W T F S S / M T W T F S S / M T W T F S S / M
1 2 / 3 4 5 6 7 8 9 / 10 11 12 13 14 15 16 / 17 18 19 20 21 22 23 / 24 25 26 27 28 29 30 / 31

2011

TODAY'S **DO OR DUE:**

Rosh Hashanah

THUR

29

FRI

30

SAT

1

OCT

SUN

2

OCT

LOOKING BACK

Check IT!

✓ I totally **aced it**
→ still in **progress**

MON	TUE	WED
26	27	28
3	4	5
10	Columbus Day 11	12
17	18	19
24	25	26 Diwali
31 Halloween	1	2

TIME
Management

Not enough time to get it all done? Although there are only 24 hours in a day, you can learn to organize and manage your time wisely. Make a list of things you need to accomplish each day and how long each task will take.

THURS	FRI	SAT	SUN
29 Rosh Hashanah	30	1	2
6	7	8 Yom Kippur	9
13	14	15	16
20	21	22	23
27	28	29	30
3	4	5	6

NOV
T W T F S S / M T W T F S S / M T W T F S S / M T W T F S S / M T W
1 2 3 4 5 6 / 7 8 9 10 11 12 13 / 14 15 16 17 18 19 20 / 21 22 23 24 25 26 27 / 28 29 30

OCTOBER

OCT S S / M T W T F S S / M T W T F S S / M T W T F S S / M T W T F S S / M
     1 2 / 3 4 5 6 7 8 9 / 10 11 12 13 14 15 16 / 17 18 19 20 21 22 23 / 24 25 26 27 28 29 30 / 31

GOALS **FTW**

MON

3

TUE

4

WED

5

TODAY'S **DO OR DUE:**

Time-Management **RESOURCES**

Juggling tasks and responsibilities can be **daunting**. You can
visit your school's academic skills center for guidance on how to manage
your time. You can also check out these online resources:

- www.google.com/calendar
- www.ulc.psu.edu/studyskills/time_management.html
- http://www.dartmouth.edu/~acskills/

NOV T W T F S S / M T W T F S S / M T W T F S S / M T W T F S S / M T W
1 2 3 4 5 6 / 7 8 9 10 11 12 13 / 14 15 16 17 18 19 20 / 21 22 23 24 25 26 27 / 28 29 30

2011

TODAY'S **DO OR DUE:**

THUR

6

FRI

7

Yom Kippur

SAT

8

SUN

9

LOOKING BACK

Check IT!

✓ I totally **aced it**
→ still in **progress**

OCTOBER

OCT S S / M T W T F S S / M T W T F S S / M T W T F S S / M T W T F S S / M
     1 2 / 3 4 5 6 7 8 9 / 10 11 12 13 14 15 16 / 17 18 19 20 21 22 23 / 24 25 26 27 28 29 30 / 31

GOALS FTW

Columbus Day   TODAY'S DO OR DUE:

MON

10

TUE

11

WED

12

PROCRASTINATION: A Time-Management Trap

Putting off studying for the test another day could lead to **stressful consequences**—late-night cram sessions, inability to retain information, or a low grade. Procrastination is typically a result of poor time management. Instead, try to set realistic goals and remind yourself of them, study in small groups to stay motivated, and break large assignments into smaller tasks.

(Source: Penn State University-University Learning Centers www.ulc.psu.edu/studyskills)

NOV T W T F S S / M T W T F S S / M T W T F S S / M T W T F S S / M T W
1 2 3 4 5 6 / 7 8 9 10 11 12 13 / 14 15 16 17 18 19 20 / 21 22 23 24 25 26 27 / 28 29 30

2011

TODAY'S **DO OR DUE:**

THUR

13

FRI

14

SAT

15

SUN

16

LOOKING BACK

Check IT!

✓ I totally **aced it**
→ still in **progress**

OCTOBER

OCT S S / M T W T F S S / M T W T F S S / M T W T F S S / M
1 2 / 3 4 5 6 7 8 9 / 10 11 12 13 14 15 16 / 17 18 19 20 21 22 23 / 24 25 26 27 28 29 30 / 31

GOALS FTW

MON
17

TUE
18

WED
19

TODAY'S DO OR DUE:

Quote **THIS!**

"Procrastination is the thief of time."

EDWARD YOUNG
English poet

NOV T W T F S S / M T W T F S S / M T W T F S S / M T W T F S S / M T W
1 2 3 4 5 6 / 7 8 9 10 11 12 13 / 14 15 16 17 18 19 20 / 21 22 23 24 25 26 27 / 28 29 30

2011

TODAY'S **DO OR DUE:**

THUR

20

FRI

21

SAT

22

SUN

23

LOOKING BACK

Check IT!

✓ I totally **aced it**
→ still in **progress**

OCTOBER

OCT 1 2 / M T W T F S S 3 4 5 6 7 8 9 / M T W T F S S 10 11 12 13 14 15 16 / M T W T F S S 17 18 19 20 21 22 23 / M T W T F S S 24 25 26 27 28 29 30 / M 31

GOALS FTW

TODAY'S **DO OR DUE:**

MON

24

TUE

25

Diwali

WED

26

Read **ON!**

Check out these titles at your school library for more time-management ideas that meet your needs:

- *Time Management for College Students: How to Manage School, Work, and Fun!* – Joel Ferrell
- *The Five-Minute Time Manager for College Students* – Ronald A. Berk
- *Studying Smart: Time Management for College Students* – Scharf-Hunt & Hait

NOV T W T F S S / M T W T F S S / M T W T F S S / M T W T F S S / M T W
1 2 3 4 5 6 / 7 8 9 10 11 12 13 / 14 15 16 17 18 19 20 / 21 22 23 24 25 26 27 / 28 29 30

2011

TODAY'S **DO OR DUE:**

THUR

27

FRI

28

SAT

29

SUN

30

LOOKING BACK

Check IT!

✓ I totally **aced it**
→ still in **progress**

31 Halloween	1	2
7 Eid al-Adha	8	9
14	15	16
21	22	23
28	29	30
5	6	7

INTELLIGENCE

How you **quantify** information, adapt to new environments, and learn from experiences are part of your intelligence. It will come in to play in college as you encounter new situations and receive, process, and apply new information on a daily basis.

THURS	FRI	SAT	SUN
3	4	5	6
10	11	12 Veterans Day	13
17	18	19	20
24 Thanksgiving Day	25	26	27 Muharram
1	2	3	4
8	9	10	11

DEC   T F S S / M T W T F S S / M T W T F S S / M T W T F S S / M T W T F S
      1 2 3 4 / 5 6 7 8 9 10 11 / 12 13 14 15 16 17 18 / 19 20 21 22 23 24 25 / 26 27 28 29 30 31

GOALS FTW

Halloween

TODAY'S **DO OR DUE:**

MON

31

OCT

TUE

1

WED

2

Intelligence **RESOURCES**

Want to learn more about **intelligence theories** and how they might apply to you? Visit these online resources:

- www.aboutintelligence.co.uk
- www.eqi.org
- www.iqtest.com

$E=mc^2$

DEC T F S S / M T W T F S S / M T W T F S S / M T W T F S S / M T W T F S
1 2 3 4 / 5 6 7 8 9 10 11 / 12 13 14 15 16 17 18 / 19 20 21 22 23 24 25 / 26 27 28 29 30 31

2011

TODAY'S **DO OR DUE:**

THUR

3

FRI

4

SAT

5

SUN

6

LOOKING BACK

Check IT!

✓ I totally **aced it**
→ still in **progress**

NOVEMBER

NOV | T W T F S S / M T W T F S S / M T W T F S S / M T W T F S S / M T W
1 2 3 4 5 6 / 7 8 9 10 11 12 13 / 14 15 16 17 18 19 20 / 21 22 23 24 25 26 27 / 28 29 30

GOALS FTW

Eid al-Adha

TODAY'S **DO OR DUE:**

MON

7

TUE

8

WED

9

I.Q. TEST: What Does it Say? *(Source: www.aboutintelligence.co.uk/what-iq.html)*

The **Intelligence Quotient**, or I.Q. test, is a standardized test that assesses a person's general intelligence. It consists of various subjects—including arithmetic, vocabulary, and similarities. The score represents how the test taker deviates from the average population. However, your score does not directly correlate with how you will succeed in college or other aspects of your life.

DEC T F S S / M T W T F S S / M T W T F S S / M T W T F S S / M T W T F S
1 2 3 4 / 5 6 7 8 9 10 11 / 12 13 14 15 16 17 18 / 19 20 21 22 23 24 25 / 26 27 28 29 30 31

2011

TODAY'S **DO OR DUE:**

THUR
10

Veterans Day

FRI
11

SAT
12

SUN
13

LOOKING BACK

Check IT!

✓ I totally **aced it**
→ still in **progress**

NOVEMBER

NOV T W T F S S / M T W T F S S / M T W T F S S / M T W T F S S / M T W
1 2 3 4 5 6 / 7 8 9 10 11 12 13 / 14 15 16 17 18 19 20 / 21 22 23 24 25 26 27 / 28 29 30

GOALS FTW

TODAY'S DO OR DUE:

MON
14

TUE
15

WED
16

LOL!

(Source: Prochnow, Herbert V. Speaker's and Toastmaster's Handbook (p 101). Prima Lifestyles, 1993.)

At a party, a man approaches a psychiatrist and asks, *"Doctor, I understand you can tell whether a person is intelligent or not by asking some very simple questions. Is that true?"*

"Yes, very simple questions," the psychiatrist replies. *"For example, Captain Cook made three voyages around the world and died on one of them. Which one?"*

"Ah, Doc," the man says. *"You know I'm no good with history."*

DEC T F S S / M T W T F S S / M T W T F S S / M T W T F S S / M T W T F S
1 2 3 4 / 5 6 7 8 9 10 11 / 12 13 14 15 16 17 18 / 19 20 21 22 23 24 25 / 26 27 28 29 30 31

2011

TODAY'S **DO OR DUE:**

THUR

17

FRI

18

SAT

19

SUN

20

LOOKING BACK

Check IT!

✓ I totally **aced it**
→ still in **progress**

NOVEMBER

NOV T W T F S S / M T W T F S S / M T W T F S S / M T W T F S S / M T W
1 2 3 4 5 6 / 7 8 9 10 11 12 13 / 14 15 16 17 18 19 20 / 21 22 23 24 25 26 27 / 28 29 30

GOALS FTW

MON

21

TUE

22

WED

23

TODAY'S DO OR DUE:

Read ON!

Want to **learn** how various aspects of your **intelligence** might come into play as a college student? Check out these titles at your school library:

- *Keys to Success: Building Successful Intelligence for College, Career, and Life* – Carol Carter, Joyce Bishop, and Sarah Lyman Kravits
- *Emotional Intelligence Leadership: A Guide for College Students* – Marcy L. Shankman and Scott J. Allen

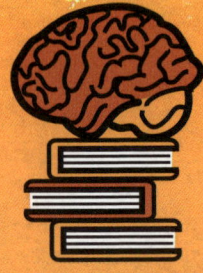

DEC T F S S / M T W T F S S / M T W T F S S / M T W T F S S / M T W T F S
     1 2 3 4 / 5 6 7 8 9 10 11 / 12 13 14 15 16 17 18 / 19 20 21 22 23 24 25 / 26 27 28 29 30 31

2011

TODAY'S **DO OR DUE:**

Thanksgiving Day

THUR

24

FRI

25

SAT

26

Muharram

SUN

27

LOOKING BACK

Check IT!

✓ I totally **aced it**
→ still in **progress**

MON	TUE	WED
28	29	30
5	6	7
12	13	14
19	20	21 Hanukkah
26 Kwanzaa	27	28
2	3	4

Critical THINKING

Critical thinkers don't just accept information for what it is—they form conclusions by combining logic with research and evaluating multiple points of view. Critical-thinking skills include processing info analytically, logically, and creatively to make rational decisions and solve problems.

THURS	FRI	SAT	SUN
1	2	3	4
8	9	10	11
15	16	17	18
22	23	24	25 Christmas Day
29	30	31	1 New Year's Day
5	6	7	8

JAN

S M T W T F S S / M T W T F S S / M T W T F S S / M T W T F S S / M T
1 2 3 4 5 6 7 8 / 9 10 11 12 13 14 15 / 16 17 18 19 20 21 22 / 23 24 25 26 27 28 29 / 30 31

177

DECEMBER

DEC

| T | F | S | S | / | M | T | W | T | F | S | S | / | M | T | W | T | F | S | S | / | M | T | W | T | F | S | S | / | M | T | W | T | F | S |
| 1 | 2 | 3 | 4 | | 5 | 6 | 7 | 8 | 9 | 10 | 11 | | 12 | 13 | 14 | 15 | 16 | 17 | 18 | | 19 | 20 | 21 | 22 | 23 | 24 | 25 | | 26 | 27 | 28 | 29 | 30 | 31 |

GOALS FTW

TODAY'S DO OR DUE:

MON

28

NOV

TUE

29

NOV

WED

30

NOV

Critical-Thinking RESOURCES

Want to learn to pry into information and think **outside the box**?
There are various resources to help. Here are a few to get you started:

- www.criticalthinking.org
- http://philosophy.hku.hk/think/
- www.asa3.org/ASA/education/think/critical.htm

TODAY'S **DO OR DUE:**

THUR

1

FRI

2

SAT

3

SUN

4

LOOKING BACK

Check IT!

✓ I totally **aced it**
→ still in **progress**

179

DECEMBER

DEC T F S S / M T W T F S S / M T W T F S S / M T W T F S S / M T W T F S
     1 2 3 4 / 5 6 7 8 9 10 11 / 12 13 14 15 16 17 18 / 19 20 21 22 23 24 25 / 26 27 28 29 30 31

GOALS FTW

TODAY'S DO OR DUE:

MON

5

TUE

6

WED

7

ANALYZE: What's the Importance?

Students who **think critically** break information into parts and examine it in detail. This way, they can determine any flaws in the information or identify other ways of thinking they may have missed if they had accepted the information at face value. Encourage yourself to continually practice critical thinking by analyzing ideas, claims, judgments, and theories presented to you!

(Source: www.criticalthinking.org)

JAN S / M T W T F S S / M T W T F S S / M T W T F S S / M T W T F S S / M T
1 2 3 4 5 6 7 8 9 10 11 12 13 14 15 16 17 18 19 20 21 22 23 24 25 26 27 28 29 30 31

2011

TODAY'S **DO OR DUE:**

THUR

8

FRI

9

SAT

10

SUN

11

LOOKING BACK

Check IT!

✓ I totally **aced it**
→ still in **progress**

DECEMBER

DEC T F S S / M T W T F S S / M T W T F S S / M T W T F S S / M T W T F S
1 2 3 4 / 5 6 7 8 9 10 11 / 12 13 14 15 16 17 18 / 19 20 21 22 23 24 25 / 26 27 28 29 30 31

GOALS FTW

MON

12

TUE

13

WED

14

TODAY'S DO OR DUE:

BRAIN TEASER

(Source: Gardner, Martin. Perplexing Puzzles & Tantalizing Teasers. Simon & Schuster Inc., 1969.)

Jim and Tom find a construction pipeline in a vacant lot. The pipe is large enough that each person can squeeze into it from one end to the other. If Jim and Tom go into the pipe from opposite ends, is it possible for each of them to crawl the entire length and come out the other end?

A. Yes, first Jim crawls through at one end. When he exits, Tom crawls through from the other end.

JAN S/MTWTFSS/MTWTFSS/MTWTFSS/MTWTFSS/MT
1 / 2 3 4 5 6 7 8 / 9 10 11 12 13 14 15 / 16 17 18 19 20 21 22 / 23 24 25 26 27 28 29 / 30 31

2011

TODAY'S **DO OR DUE:**

THUR

15

FRI

16

SAT

17

SUN

18

LOOKING BACK

Check IT!

✓ I totally **aced it**
→ still in **progress**

DECEMBER

DEC
| T | F | S | S | / | M | T | W | T | F | S | S | / | M | T | W | T | F | S | S | / | M | T | W | T | F | S | S | / | M | T | W | T | F | S |
| 1 | 2 | 3 | 4 | | 5 | 6 | 7 | 8 | 9 | 10 | 11 | | 12 | 13 | 14 | 15 | 16 | 17 | 18 | | 19 | 20 | 21 | 22 | 23 | 24 | 25 | | 26 | 27 | 28 | 29 | 30 | 31 |

GOALS **FTW**

TODAY'S **DO OR DUE:**

MON
19

TUE
20

Hanukkah

WED
21

Read **ON!**

It takes **practice** to become a strong critical thinker. For some guidance, check out these titles at your school library:

- *Asking the Right Questions: A Guide to Critical Thinking* – Neil Browne and Stuart M. Keeley
- *Critical Thinking & Logic Skills for College Students* – Elizabeth L. Chesla
- *Study and Critical Thinking Skills in College* – Kathleen T. McWhorter

JAN S / M T W T F S S / M T W T F S S / M T W T F S S / M T W T F S S / M T
1 2 3 4 5 6 7 8   9 10 11 12 13 14 15   16 17 18 19 20 21 22   23 24 25 26 27 28 29   30 31

2011

TODAY'S **DO OR DUE:**

THUR

22

FRI

23

SAT

24

Christmas Day

SUN

25

LOOKING BACK

Check IT!

✓ I totally **aced it**
→ still in **progress**

DECEMBER

GOALS FTW

Kwanzaa   TODAY'S **DO OR DUE:**

MON

26

TUE

27

WED

28

JAN S / M T W T F S S / M T W T F S S / M T W T F S S / M T W T F S S / M T
1   2 3 4 5 6 7 8   9 10 11 12 13 14 15   16 17 18 19 20 21 22   23 24 25 26 27 28 29   30 31

2011

TODAY'S **DO OR DUE:**

THUR
29

FRI
30

SAT
31

New Year's Day

SUN
1

JAN

LOOKING BACK

Check IT!
✓ I totally **aced it**
→ still in **progress**

MON	TUE	WED
26 Kwanzaa	27	28
2	3	4
9	10	11
16 Martin Luther King, Jr. Day	17	18
23 Chinese New Year	24	25
30	31	1

Note-TAKING

Note-taking skills are **essential** for **college success!** Write down the main points, key vocabulary terms, important facts, and formulas—be sure to review them after class and fill in missing information!

THURS	FRI	SAT	SUN
29	30	31	1 New Year's Day
5	6	7	8
12	13	14	15
19	20	21	22
26	27	28	29
2	3	4	5

FEB

W	T	F	S	S	/	M	T	W	T	F	S	S	/	M	T	W	T	F	S	S	/	M	T	W	T	F	S	S	/	M	T	W
1	2	3	4	5		6	7	8	9	10	11	12		13	14	15	16	17	18	19		20	21	22	23	24	25	26		27	28	29

JANUARY

GOALS FTW

TODAY'S **DO OR DUE:**

MON

2

TUE

3

WED

4

Note-Taking **RESOURCES**

Having trouble finding information from your notes? **Get organized!**
Seek help from your school's academic skills center and visit these
online resources:

- www.collegeboard.com/student/plan/college-success/955.html
- www.brookhavencollege.edu/studentsvcs/counseling/note-taking.aspx
- www.wikihow.com/Take-Lecture-Notes

FEB W T F S S / M T W T F S S / M T W T F S S / M T W T F S S / M T W
1 2 3 4 5 / 6 7 8 9 10 11 12 / 13 14 15 16 17 18 19 / 20 21 22 23 24 25 26 / 27 28 29

2012

TODAY'S **DO OR DUE:**

THUR

5

FRI

6

SAT

7

SUN

8

LOOKING BACK

Check IT!

✓ I totally **aced it**

→ still in **progress**

JANUARY

JAN S / M T W T F S S / M T W T F S S / M T W T F S S / M T W T F S S / M T
1 / 2 3 4 5 6 7 8 / 9 10 11 12 13 14 15 / 16 17 18 19 20 21 22 / 23 24 25 26 27 28 29 / 30 31

GOALS **FTW**

TODAY'S **DO OR DUE:**

MON

9

TUE

10

WED

11

METHODS: Finding a System for You

(Source: http://sas.calpoly.edu/asc/ssl/notetaking.systems.html)

There's more to **note-taking** than writing information on paper—keep it organized by finding a method that works best for you! The Cornell, Outline, Mapping, Charting, and Sentence methods are the same in that they organize your notes in an easy-to-review format. Each system varies, however, with how the information is laid out on paper.

FEB WTFSS / MTWTFSS / MTWTFSS / MTWTFSS / MTW
1 2 3 4 5 / 6 7 8 9 10 11 12 / 13 14 15 16 17 18 19 / 20 21 22 23 24 25 26 / 27 28 29

2012

TODAY'S **DO OR DUE:**

THUR

12

FRI

13

SAT

14

SUN

15

LOOKING BACK

Check IT!

✓ I totally **aced it**
→ still in **progress**

JANUARY

JAN S / M T W T F S S / M T W T F S S / M T W T F S S / M T W T F S S / M T
1 / 2 3 4 5 6 7 8 / 9 10 11 12 13 14 15 / 16 17 18 19 20 21 22 / 23 24 25 26 27 28 29 / 30 31

GOALS FTW

Martin Luther King, Jr. Day

TODAY'S **DO OR DUE:**

MON

16

TUE

17

WED

18

QUICK TIPS: Note-Taking Strategies

(Source: www.collegeboard.com/ student/plan/college-success/955.html)

- **Stay Organized** – Keep notes in one place; date and number pages.
- **Before Class** – Review materials and bring a list of questions you may have.
- **During Class** – Find a note-taking method that works for you. Don't write every word, indicate main points as you go, and ask questions.
- **After Class** – Review, highlight, and fill in missing material.

FEB

W T F S S / M T W T F S S / M T W T F S S / M T W T F S S / M T W
1 2 3 4 5 / 6 7 8 9 10 11 12 / 13 14 15 16 17 18 19 / 20 21 22 23 24 25 26 / 27 28 29

2012

TODAY'S **DO OR DUE:**

THUR

19

FRI

20

SAT

21

SUN

22

LOOKING BACK

Check IT!

✓ I totally **aced it**
→ still in **progress**

JANUARY

JAN S / M T W T F S S / M T W T F S S / M T W T F S S / M T W T F S S / M T
     1 / 2 3 4 5 6 7 8 / 9 10 11 12 13 14 15 / 16 17 18 19 20 21 22 / 23 24 25 26 27 28 29 / 30 31

GOALS FTW

Chinese New Year

TODAY'S **DO OR DUE:**

MON

23

TUE

24

WED

25

Read ON!

Haven't established a **note-taking strategy** yet? Get started with advice and techniques from the experts! Look for these titles at your school library:

- *Take Notes* – Ron Fry
- *Note-Taking Made Easy* – Judi Kesselman-Turkel and Franklynn Peterson
- *Speedwriting for Note-Taking and Study Skills* – Joe Pullis

FEB W T F S S / M T W T F S S / M T W T F S S / M T W T F S S / M T W
1 2 3 4 5 / 6 7 8 9 10 11 12 / 13 14 15 16 17 18 19 / 20 21 22 23 24 25 26 / 27 28 29

2012

TODAY'S **DO OR DUE:**

THUR

26

FRI

27

SAT

28

SUN

29

LOOKING BACK

Check IT!

✓ I totally **aced it**
→ still in **progress**

	MON	TUE	WED
	30	31	1
	6	7	8
	13	14 Valentine's Day	15
	20 Presidents' Day	21	22
	27	28	29
	5	6	7

TEST-
Taking

Test results help professors assess students' **understanding** of course material. Review key elements from lecture notes and assigned readings to prepare for test day. Afterward, review your preparation techniques and identify strategies that worked and replace those that didn't.

THURS	FRI	SAT	SUN
2	3	4	5
9	10	11	12
16	17	18	19
23	24	25	26
1	2	3	4
8	9	10	11

MAR T F S S / M T W T F S S / M T W T F S S / M T W T F S S / M T W T F S
1 2 3 4 / 5 6 7 8 9 10 11 / 12 13 14 15 16 17 18 / 19 20 21 22 23 24 25 / 26 27 28 29 30 31

FEBRUARY

GOALS FTW

MON

30

JAN

TUE

31

JAN

WED

1

TODAY'S DO OR DUE:

Test-Taking RESOURCES

Need to brush up on your **test-taking strategies** but not sure where to begin? Your academic skills center can help! There are also online resources to get you started:

- www.isu.edu/advising/tips_testing.shtml
- www.testtakingtips.com/
- Read *Test-Taking Strategies* for free at www.books.google.com

MAR

T F S S / M T W T F S S / M T W T F S S / M T W T F S S / M T W T F S
1 2 3 4 / 5 6 7 8 9 10 11 / 12 13 14 15 16 17 18 / 19 20 21 22 23 24 25 / 26 27 28 29 30 31

2012

TODAY'S **DO OR DUE:**

THUR

2

FRI

3

SAT

4

SUN

5

LOOKING BACK

Check IT!

✓ I totally **aced it**
→ still in **progress**

FEBRUARY

FEB W T F S S / M T W T F S S / M T W T F S S / M T W T F S S / M T W
1 2 3 4 5 / 6 7 8 9 10 11 12 / 13 14 15 16 17 18 19 / 20 21 22 23 24 25 26 / 27 28 29

GOALS **FTW**

TODAY'S **DO OR DUE:**

MON

6

TUE

7

WED

8

ANXIETY: A Stressful Situation

*(Source: www.kidshealth.org/teen/
school_jobs/school/test_anxiety.html#)*

It happens each **test day**—your heart races, your stomach flutters, and you may even feel sick. Test anxiety is a form of performance anxiety and is sometimes fueled by negative thoughts or worry. Fortunately, being prepared, having positive thoughts, and accepting mistakes can help alleviate the stress.

MAR T F S S / M T W T F S S / M T W T F S S / M T W T F S S / M T W T F S
1 2 3 4 / 5 6 7 8 9 10 11 / 12 13 14 15 16 17 18 / 19 20 21 22 23 24 25 / 26 27 28 29 30 31

2012

TODAY'S **DO OR DUE:**

THUR

9

FRI

10

SAT

11

SUN

12

LOOKING BACK

Check IT!

✓ I totally **aced it**
→ still in **progress**

FEBRUARY

GOALS FTW

MON

13

Valentine's Day

TUE

14

WED

15

TODAY'S DO OR DUE:

QUICK TIPS: Surviving the Test

(Source: www.collegeboard.com/student/ plan/boost-your-skills/10296.html)

- Eat well before the test.
- Review the test before you start.
- Read all directions carefully.
- Answer easy questions first—but answer all of them.
- Ask questions if something isn't clear.
- Identify key words that will help you.
- Rewrite questions if they don't make sense.
- If you finish early, use remaining time to check your answers.

MAR
T F S S / M T W T F S S / M T W T F S S / M T W T F S S / M T W T F S
1 2 3 4 / 5 6 7 8 9 10 11 / 12 13 14 15 16 17 18 / 19 20 21 22 23 24 25 / 26 27 28 29 30 31

2012

TODAY'S **DO OR DUE:**

THUR

16

FRI

17

SAT

18

SUN

19

LOOKING BACK

Check IT!

✓ I totally **aced it**
→ still in **progress**

FEBRUARY

GOALS FTW

Presidents' Day   TODAY'S DO OR DUE:

MON

20

TUE

21

WED

22

Read ON!

Find ways to tackle **test anxiety** or improve your test-taking strategies by looking for these titles at your school library:

- *The Anxious Test-Taker's Guide to Cracking Any Test* – Princeton Review
- *Test-Taking Power Strategies* – Learning Express
- *Test-Taking Secrets: Study Better, Test Smarter, and Get Great Grades* – Steven Frank

MAR T F S S / M T W T F S S / M T W T F S S / M T W T F S S / M T W T F S
1 2 3 4 / 5 6 7 8 9 10 11 / 12 13 14 15 16 17 18 / 19 20 21 22 23 24 25 / 26 27 28 29 30 31

2012

TODAY'S **DO OR DUE:**

THUR

23

FRI

24

SAT

25

SUN

26

LOOKING BACK

Check IT!

✓ I totally **aced it**
→ still in **progress**

27	28	29
5	6	7
12	13	14
19	20	21
26	27	28
2	3	4

Majors &
CAREERS

So you think it would be **fun** to be a lawyer, graphic designer, or biologist? How will you decide which career is right for you before enduring extensive postsecondary training? The staff at your campus career center will help you find resources to help determine your path.

THURS	FRI	SAT	SUN
1	2	3	4
8	9	10	11
15	16	17	18
22	23	24	25
29	30	31	1
5	6 Good Friday	7 Passover	8 Easter

APR

	S	M	T	W	T	F	S	S	M	T	W	T	F	S	S	M	T	W	T	F	S	S	M	T	W	T	F	S	S	M
	1	2	3	4	5	6	7	8	9	10	11	12	13	14	15	16	17	18	19	20	21	22	23	24	25	26	27	28	29	30

209

GOALS FTW

MON

27

FEB

TUE

28

FEB

WED

29

FEB

TODAY'S DO OR DUE:

Majors & Careers RESOURCES

Declaring a **major** and selecting a **career path** can be a challenging decision. There are a number of online resources to help you kick around ideas. Here are a few to get you started:

- www.princetonreview.com/majors.aspx
- www.collegeboard.com/student/csearch/majors_careers/
- www.collegemajors101.com/

APR S / M T W T F S S / M T W T F S S / M T W T F S S / M T W T F S S / M
1 / 2 3 4 5 6 7 8 / 9 10 11 12 13 14 15 / 16 17 18 19 20 21 22 / 23 24 25 26 27 28 29 / 30

2012

TODAY'S **DO OR DUE:**

THUR

1

FRI

2

SAT

3

SUN

4

LOOKING BACK

Check IT!

✓ I totally **aced it**
→ still in **progress**

MARCH

MAR
T F S S / M T W T F S S / M T W T F S S / M T W T F S S / M T W T F S
1 2 3 4 / 5 6 7 8 9 10 11 / 12 13 14 15 16 17 18 / 19 20 21 22 23 24 25 / 26 27 28 29 30 31

GOALS FTW

MON
5

TUE
6

WED
7

TODAY'S DO OR DUE:

INTERNSHIPS: A Sneak Preview

A college internship is a great way to gain **valuable work experience** in your area of study. It's also a great way to determine if you still want to pursue that career. Internships are often unpaid, but many students find internships that pay either a stipend or another form of salary. Visit your school's career center for internship opportunities.

APR S / M T W T F S S / M T W T F S S / M T W T F S S / M T W T F S S / M
1 / 2 3 4 5 6 7 8 / 9 10 11 12 13 14 15 / 16 17 18 19 20 21 22 / 23 24 25 26 27 28 29 / 30

2012

TODAY'S **DO OR DUE:**

THUR

8

FRI

9

SAT

10

SUN

11

LOOKING BACK

Check IT!

✓ I totally **aced it**
→ still in **progress**

MARCH.

MAR **T F S S** / **M T W T F S S** / **M T W T F S S** / **M T W T F S S** / **M T W T F S**
1 2 3 4 / 5 6 7 8 9 10 11 / 12 13 14 15 16 17 18 / 19 20 21 22 23 24 25 / 26 27 28 29 30 31

GOALS FTW

MON

12

TUE

13

WED

14

TODAY'S **DO OR DUE:**

FAST FACTS: Popular Majors

According to the **National Center for Educational Statistics**, in the 2006-07 school year, the largest numbers of bachelor's degrees were awarded in:

- Business
- Social Sciences & History
- Education
- Health Sciences

APR S / M T W T F S S / M T W T F S S / M T W T F S S / M T W T F S S / M
1 / 2 3 4 5 6 7 8 / 9 10 11 12 13 14 15 / 16 17 18 19 20 21 22 / 23 24 25 26 27 28 29 / 30

2012

TODAY'S **DO OR DUE:**

THUR

15

FRI

16

SAT

17

SUN

18

LOOKING BACK

Check IT!

✓ I totally **aced it**
→ still in **progress**

MARCH

MAR | T F S S / M T W T F S S / M T W T F S S / M T W T F S S / M T W T F S
1 2 3 4 / 5 6 7 8 9 10 11 / 12 13 14 15 16 17 18 / 19 20 21 22 23 24 25 / 26 27 28 29 30 31

GOALS FTW

TODAY'S **DO OR DUE:**

MON

19

TUE

20

WED

21

Read ON!

Not sure what **major** to pursue? Look for these titles at your library:

- *50 Best Jobs for Your Personality* – Michael Farr and Laurence Shatkin
- *College Majors Handbook with Real Career Paths and Payoff* – Neeta P. Fogg, Paul Harrington, and Thomas Harrington
- *College Majors & Careers: A Resource Guide for Effective Life Planning* – Paul Phifer

APR S/MTWTFSS/MTWTFSS/MTWTFSS/MTWTFSS/M
1 / 2 3 4 5 6 7 8 / 9 10 11 12 13 14 15 / 16 17 18 19 20 21 22 / 23 24 25 26 27 28 29 / 30

2012

TODAY'S **DO OR DUE:**

THUR

22

FRI

23

SAT

24

SUN

25

LOOKING BACK

Check IT!

✓ I totally **aced it**
→ still in **progress**

MARCH

GOALS **FTW**

TODAY'S **DO OR DUE:**

MON

26

TUE

27

WED

28

Quote THIS!

"The best career advice to give to the young is 'Find out what you like doing best and get someone to pay you for doing it.'"

KATHERINE WHITEHORN
British journalist

APR   S / M T W T F S S / M T W T F S S / M T W T F S S / M T W T F S S / M
     1 / 2 3 4 5 6 7 8 / 9 10 11 12 13 14 15 / 16 17 18 19 20 21 22 / 23 24 25 26 27 28 29 / 30

2012

TODAY'S **DO OR DUE:**

THUR

29

FRI

30

SAT

31

SUN

1

APR

LOOKING BACK

Check IT!

✓ I totally **aced it**
→ still in **progress**

MON	TUE	WED
26	27	28
2	3	4
9	10	11
16	17	18
23	24	25
30	1	2

Reading and **WRITING**

You use your reading and writing skills **every day**—both in and outside the classroom. Strong literacy skills help you to effectively communicate with others and interpret the world. Your future depends on your ability to read and write well—use your time in college to improve these skills!

THURS	FRI	SAT	SUN
29	30	31	1
5	6	7 Passover	8 Easter

Good Friday

12	13	14	15
19	20	21	22
26	27	28	29

Vesak

| 3 | 4 | 5 | 6 |

MAY

T	W	T	F	S	S	/	M	T	W	T	F	S	S	/	M	T	W	T	F	S	S	/	M	T	W	T	F	S	S	/	M	T	W	T
1	2	3	4	5	6		7	8	9	10	11	12	13		14	15	16	17	18	19	20		21	22	23	24	25	26	27		28	29	30	31

APRIL

APR S / M T W T F S S / M T W T F S S / M T W T F S S / M T W T F S S / M
1 / 2 3 4 5 6 7 8 / 9 10 11 12 13 14 15 / 16 17 18 19 20 21 22 / 23 24 25 26 27 28 29 / 30

GOALS **FTW**

TODAY'S **DO OR DUE:**

MON

2

TUE

3

WED

4

Reading and Writing **RESOURCES**

Need to harness **efficient** reading and writing skills for college?
Visit your school's writing center for help. You can also find resources online!
Here are a few to get you started:

- www.collegeboard.com/student/plan/boost-your-skills/index.html
- writing-program.uchicago.edu/resources/collegewriting/
- http://www.dartmouth.edu/~acskills/

MAY T W T F S S / M T W T F S S / M T W T F S S / M T W T F S S / M T W T
1 2 3 4 5 6 / 7 8 9 10 11 12 13 / 14 15 16 17 18 19 20 / 21 22 23 24 25 26 27 / 28 29 30 31

2012

TODAY'S **DO OR DUE:**

THUR

5

Good Friday

FRI

6

Passover

SAT

7

Easter

SUN

8

LOOKING BACK

Check IT!

✓ I totally **aced it**
→ still in **progress**

APRIL

APR

S / M T W T F S S / M T W T F S S / M T W T F S S / M T W T F S S / M
1 / 2 3 4 5 6 7 8 / 9 10 11 12 13 14 15 / 16 17 18 19 20 21 22 / 23 24 25 26 27 28 29 / 30

GOALS FTW

TODAY'S DO OR DUE:

MON

9

TUE

10

WED

11

SQ3R: Efficient Textbook Reading

(Source: www.collegeboard.com/student/ plan/college-success/26666.html)

With **so many** reading assignments in such a short time, **it's important** to read efficiently and effectively. The Survey, Question, Read, Recite, and Review method, called SQ3R, is a proven technique used to sharpen college reading skills—especially for reading textbooks! Previewing the material, formulating questions, and immediately reviewing content should prove helpful when conquering varied, often complicated, reading assignments.

MAY T W T F S S / M T W T F S S / M T W T F S S / M T W T F S S / M T W T
1 2 3 4 5 6 / 7 8 9 10 11 12 13 / 14 15 16 17 18 19 20 / 21 22 23 24 25 26 27 / 28 29 30 31

2012

TODAY'S **DO OR DUE:**

THUR

12

FRI

13

SAT

14

SUN

15

LOOKING BACK

Check IT!

✓ I totally **aced it**
→ still in **progress**

APRIL

APR S / M I W i F O O / M T W T F S S / M T W T F S S / M T W T F S S / M
1 / 2 3 4 5 6 7 8 / 9 10 11 12 13 14 15 / 16 17 18 19 20 21 22 / 23 24 25 26 27 28 29 / 30

GOALS FTW

TODAY'S DO OR DUE:

MON

16

TUE

17

WED

18

Quote THIS!

"My aim is to put down what I see and what I feel
in the best and simplest way I can tell it."

ERNEST HEMINGWAY
American writer

MAY T W T F S S / M T W T F S S / M T W T F S S / M T W T F S S / M T W T
1 2 3 4 5 6 / 7 8 9 10 11 12 13 / 14 15 16 17 18 19 20 / 21 22 23 24 25 26 27 / 28 29 30 31

2012

TODAY'S **DO OR DUE:**

THUR

19

FRI

20

SAT

21

SUN

22

LOOKING BACK

Check IT!

✓ I totally **aced it**
→ still in **progress**

APRIL

APR S / M T W T F S S / M T W T F S S / M T W T F S S / M T W T F S S / M
1 / 2 3 4 5 6 7 8 / 9 10 11 12 13 14 15 / 16 17 18 19 20 21 22 / 23 24 25 26 27 28 29 / 30

GOALS FTW

TODAY'S **DO OR DUE:**

MON

23

TUE

24

WED

25

Read **ON!**

Find **new techniques** to help you **study** and **communicate** more efficiently. Check out these book titles at your school library:
- *Ten Steps to Improving College Reading Skills* – John Langan
- *Making Connections: Study Skills, Reading, and Writing* – Ann Dillon
- *What it Takes: Writing in College* – Laurence Behrens

MAY T W T F S S / M T W T F S S / M T W T F S S / M T W T F S S / M T W T
1 2 3 4 5 6 / 7 8 9 10 11 12 13 / 14 15 16 17 18 19 20 / 21 22 23 24 25 26 27 / 28 29 30 31

2012

TODAY'S **DO OR DUE:**

THUR

26

FRI

27

Vesak

SAT

28

SUN

29

LOOKING BACK

Check IT!

✓ I totally **aced it**
→ still in **progress**

MON	TUE	WED
30	1	2
7	8	9
14	15	16
21	22	23
28	Memorial Day 29	30
4	5	6

A+

SPEAKING

Verbal communication is essential—often comprising a portion of your class grade in the form of discussions and presentations. Public speaking is important to understanding and being understood by others. Gain confidence and improve your speaking skills by taking a public speaking course.

THURS	FRI	SAT	SUN
3	4	5	6
10	11	12	13 Mother's Day
17	18	19	20
24	25	26	27
31	1	2	3
7	8	9	10

JUNE F S S / M T W T F S S / M T W T F S S / M T W T F S S / M T W T F S
1 2 3 / 4 5 6 7 8 9 10 / 11 12 13 14 15 16 17 / 18 19 20 21 22 23 24 / 25 26 27 28 29 30

MAY

T W T F S S / M T W T F S S / M T W T F S S / M T W T F S S / M T W T
1 2 3 4 5 6 / 7 8 9 10 11 12 13 / 14 15 16 17 18 19 20 / 21 22 23 24 25 26 27 / 28 29 30 31

GOALS FTW

TODAY'S **DO OR DUE:**

MON

30

APR

TUE

1

WED

2

Speaking **RESOURCES**

Looking for ways to **improve** your public speaking skills?
You can always enroll in a public speaking course or join the debate
team. Get a jump start by visiting these online resources:

• www.toastmasters.org
• www.glossophobia.com

JUNE | F S S / M T W T F S S / M T W T F S S / M T W T F S S / M T W T F S
1 2 3 / 4 5 6 7 8 9 10 / 11 12 13 14 15 16 17 / 18 19 20 21 22 23 24 / 25 26 27 28 29 30

2012

TODAY'S **DO OR DUE:**

THUR

3

FRI

4

SAT

5

SUN

6

LOOKING BACK

Check IT!

✓ I totally **aced it**
→ still in **progress**

MAY

MAY
T W T F S S / M T W T F S S / M T W T F S S / M T W T F S S / M T W T
1 2 3 4 5 6 / 7 8 9 10 11 12 13 / 14 15 16 17 18 19 20 / 21 22 23 24 25 26 27 / 28 29 30 31

GOALS **FTW**

TODAY'S **DO OR DUE:**

MON

7

TUE

8

WED

9

Quote **THIS!**

"Preparing and writing a speech, delivering it, and realizing that it does not have to be an ordeal: It is an opportunity, and if the opportunity is grasped and the response is the one hoped for, it can be immediately satisfying—even a pleasure."

EDWIN NEWMAN
former NBC News correspondent

JUNE F S S / M T W T F S S / M T W T F S S / M T W T F S S / M T W T F S
1 2 3 / 4 5 6 7 8 9 10 / 11 12 13 14 15 16 17 / 18 19 20 21 22 23 24 / 25 26 27 28 29 30

2012

TODAY'S **DO OR DUE:**

THUR

10

FRI

11

SAT

12

Mother's Day

SUN

13

LOOKING BACK

Check IT!

✓ I totally **aced it**
→ still in **progress**

MAY

MAY T W T F S S / M T W T F S S / M T W T F S S / M T W T F S S / M T W T
1 2 3 4 5 6 / 7 8 9 10 11 12 13 / 14 15 16 17 18 19 20 / 21 22 23 24 25 26 27 / 28 29 30 31

GOALS FTW

TODAY'S DO OR DUE:

MON

14

TUE

15

WED

16

FAST FACTS: Public Speaking Myths

(Source: Krannich, Caryl Rae. 101 Secrets of Highly Effective Speakers (p 4). Impact Publications, 2004.)

- The more notes you have at the podium, the better you will present your speech.
- You can dress however you would like for your presentation, as long as you give a good speech.
- Practicing your speech is not a good idea; it's better if the material is fresh.
- Feeling nervous before speaking will hinder your presentation.

236

JUNE | F S S / M T W T F S S / M T W T F S S / M T W T F S S / M T W T F S
1 2 3 / 4 5 6 7 8 9 10 / 11 12 13 14 15 16 17 / 18 19 20 21 22 23 24 / 25 26 27 28 29 30

2012

TODAY'S **DO OR DUE:**

THUR

17

FRI

18

SAT

19

SUN

20

LOOKING BACK

Check IT!

✓ I totally **aced it**
→ still in **progress**

MAY

MAY | T W T F S S / M T W T F S S / M T W T F S S / M T W T F S S / M T W T
1 2 3 4 5 6 / 7 8 9 10 11 12 13 / 14 15 16 17 18 19 20 / 21 22 23 24 25 26 27 / 28 29 30 31

GOALS FTW

TODAY'S DO OR DUE:

MON

21

TUE

22

WED

23

Read ON!

Verbal communication is usually a **requirement** for college courses and in most careers. Prepare for it by checking for these titles at your school library:

- *Public Speaking for College & Career* – Hamilton Gregory
- *Confessions of a Public Speaker* – Scott Berkun
- *The Confident Speaker: Beat Your Nerves and Communicate Your Best in Any Situation* – Harrison Monarth and Larina Kase

JUNE F S S / M T W T F S S / M T W T F S S / M T W T F S S / M T W T F S
1 2 3 / 4 5 6 7 8 9 10 / 11 12 13 14 15 16 17 / 18 19 20 21 22 23 24 / 25 26 27 28 29 30

2012

TODAY'S **DO OR DUE:**

THUR

24

FRI

25

SAT

26

SUN

27

LOOKING BACK

Check IT!

✓ I totally **aced it**
→ still in **progress**

MON	TUE	WED
28 Memorial Day	29	30
4	5	6
11	12	13
18	19	20
25	26	27
2	3	4 Independence Day

HEALTH

Staying healthy is crucial to your success as a student, but can often be a challenge while juggling the demands of college life. There are ways to maintain your health on campus—scheduling time for adequate rest, fitting in time to exercise, eating sensibly, and learning relaxation techniques will help!

THURS	FRI	SAT	SUN
31	1	2	3
7	8	9	10
14	15	16	17 Father's Day
21	22	23	24
28	29	30	1
5	6	7	8

JUN S / M T W T F S S / M T W T F S S / M T W T F S S / M T W T F S S / M T
1 / 2 3 4 5 6 7 8 / 9 10 11 12 13 14 15 / 16 17 18 19 20 21 22 / 23 24 25 26 27 28 29 / 30 31

JUNE

JUN
F S S / M T W T F S S / M T W T F S S / M T W T F S S / M T W T F S
1 2 3 / 4 5 6 7 8 9 10 / 11 12 13 14 15 16 17 / 18 19 20 21 22 23 24 / 25 26 27 28 29 30

GOALS FTW

Memorial Day

TODAY'S **DO OR DUE:**

MON

28

MAY

TUE

29

MAY

WED

30

MAY

HEALTH Resources

It is possible to juggle the demands of college classes and campus life. Visit these online resources for tips to stay healthy on campus:

- www.revolutionhealth.com/conditions/mental-behavioral-health/college-health/
- www.cdc.gov/family/college/
- www.gocollege.com/survival/college-health.html

JUL S / M T W T F S S / M T W T F S S / M T W T F S S / M T W T F S S / M T
1 / 2 3 4 5 6 7 8 / 9 10 11 12 13 14 15 / 16 17 18 19 20 21 22 / 23 24 25 26 27 28 29 / 30 31

2012

TODAY'S **DO OR DUE:**

THUR

31

MAY

FRI

1

SAT

2

SUN

3

LOOKING BACK

Check IT!

✓ I totally **aced it**
→ still in **progress**

JUNE

JUN F S S / M T W T F S S / M T W T F S S / M T W T F S S / M T W T F S
1 2 3 / 4 5 6 7 8 9 10 / 11 12 13 14 15 16 17 / 18 19 20 21 22 23 24 / 25 26 27 28 29 30

GOALS FTW

TODAY'S DO OR DUE:

MON

4

TUE

5

WED

6

GOALS FTW

EXERCISE: What are the Benefits?

Regular exercise improves physical and mental health!
Reduced stress, enhanced mood, and improved energy are a few of the benefits. It's recommended to engage in physical activity that increases your breathing and heart rates for at least one hour several times each week. Brisk walking, jogging, or aerobics are common forms of exercise.

JUL S / M T W T F S S / M T W T F S S / M T W T F S S / M T W T F S S / M T
1 / 2 3 4 5 6 7 8 / 9 10 11 12 13 14 15 / 16 17 18 19 20 21 22 / 23 24 25 26 27 28 29 / 30 31

2012

TODAY'S **DO OR DUE:**

THUR

7

FRI

8

SAT

9

SUN

10

LOOKING BACK

Check IT!

✓ I totally **aced it**
→ still in **progress**

JUNE

JUN

F S S / M T W T F S S / M T W T F S S / M T W T F S S / M T W T F S
1 2 3 / 4 5 6 7 8 9 10 / 11 12 13 14 15 16 17 / 18 19 20 21 22 23 24 / 25 26 27 28 29 30

GOALS FTW

MON

11

TUE

12

WED

13

TODAY'S DO OR DUE:

FAST FACTS: Health Alert!

(Sources: www.campuscalm.com/did_you_know.html, www.halfofus.com/_media/_mr/may09/exec.pdf)

According to a poll conducted by The Associated Press and MTVU:

- 85% of students polled reported they felt stressed on a daily basis.
- Six out of ten students said stress prevented them from completing their work more than once.
- Over 70% of the students polled did not consider meeting with a counselor to deal with their stress or other emotional issues.

JUL S/M T W T F S S/M T W T F S S/M T W T F S S/M T W T F S S/M T
1 / 2 3 4 5 6 7 8 / 9 10 11 12 13 14 15 / 16 17 18 19 20 21 22 / 23 24 25 26 27 28 29 / 30 31

2012

TODAY'S **DO OR DUE:**

THUR

14

FRI

15

SAT

16

Father's Day

SUN

17

LOOKING BACK

Check IT!

✓ I totally **aced it**
→ still in **progress**

JUNE

JUN
F S S / M T W T F S S / M T W T F S S / M T W T F S S / M T W T F S
1 2 3 / 4 5 6 7 8 9 10 / 11 12 13 14 15 16 17 / 18 19 20 21 22 23 24 / 25 26 27 28 29 30

GOALS FTW

TODAY'S **DO OR DUE:**

MON

18

TUE

19

WED

20

Read ON!

Is your **health** lagging during your busy college schedule?
Take charge—seek help by checking for these titles at your school library:

• *The Smart Student's Guide to Healthy Living: How to Survive Stress, Late Nights, and the College Cafeteria* – M. J. Smith and Fred Smith
• *Mindful Eating 101: A Guide to Healthy Eating in College and Beyond* – Susan Albers

JUL S / M T W T F S S / M T W T F S S / M T W T F S S / M T W T F S S / M T
1 / 2 3 4 5 6 7 8 / 9 10 11 12 13 14 15 / 16 17 18 19 20 21 22 / 23 24 25 26 27 28 29 / 30 31

2012

TODAY'S **DO OR DUE:**

THUR

21

FRI

22

SAT

23

SUN

24

LOOKING BACK

Check IT!

✓ I totally **aced it**
→ still in **progress**

JUNE

GOALS **FTW**

MON
25

TUE
26

WED
27

TODAY'S **DO OR DUE:**

Quote **THIS!**

"A man too busy to take care of his health is like a mechanic too busy to take care of his tools."

SPANISH PROVERB

JUL S / M T W T F S S / M T W T F S S / M T W T F S S / M T W T F S S / M T
       1 / 2 3 4 5 6 7 8 / 9 10 11 12 13 14 15 / 16 17 18 19 20 21 22 / 23 24 25 26 27 28 29 / 30 31

2012

TODAY'S **DO OR DUE:**

THUR

28

FRI

29

SAT

30

SUN

1

JUL

LOOKING BACK

Check IT!

✓ I totally **aced it**
→ still in **progress**

MON	TUE	WED
25	26	27
2	3	4 Independence Day
9	10	11
16	17	18
23	24	25
30	31	1

Self-**ASSESSMENT**

Before you select a **career** to pursue you have to **discover** who you are—your skills, interests, and abilities. Take a full-scale personality/career test to help assess your direction. Common self-assessment tests include the Myers-Briggs Type Indicator®, Enneagram® , and the MAPP™.

THURS	FRI	SAT	SUN
28	29	30	1
5	6	7	8
12	13	14	15
19	20	21 Ramadan	22
26	27	28	29
2	3	4	5

AUG W T F S S / M T W T F S S / M T W T F S S / M T W T F S S / M T W T F
1 2 3 4 5 / 6 7 8 9 10 11 12 / 13 14 15 16 17 18 19 / 20 21 22 23 24 25 26 / 27 28 29 30 31

S / M T W T F S S / M T W T F S S / M T W T F S S / M T W T F S S / M T
1 / 2 3 4 5 6 7 8 / 9 10 11 12 13 14 15 / 16 17 18 19 20 21 22 / 23 24 25 26 27 28 29 / 30 31

GOALS **FTW**

MON

2

TUE

3

Independence Day

WED

4

TODAY'S **DO OR DUE:**

Self-Assessment **RESOURCES**

Discovering your strengths, weaknesses, and interests will help you pinpoint a career path. Online resources can help you make the right decision:

• www.myersbriggs.org/
• www.careercolleges.com/career-assessment-test.jsp

AUG W T F S S / M T W T F S S / M T W T F S S / M T W T F S S / M T W T F
1 2 3 4 5 / 6 7 8 9 10 11 12 / 13 14 15 16 17 18 19 / 20 21 22 23 24 25 26 / 27 28 29 30 31

2012

TODAY'S **DO OR DUE:**

THUR

5

FRI

6

SAT

7

SUN

8

LOOKING BACK

Check IT!

✓ I totally **aced it**
→ still in **progress**

JULY

| S | / | M | T | W | T | F | S | S | / | M | T | W | T | F | S | S | / | M | T | W | T | F | S | S | / | M | T | W | T | F | S | S | / | M | T |
| 1 | | 2 | 3 | 4 | 5 | 6 | 7 | 8 | | 9 | 10 | 11 | 12 | 13 | 14 | 15 | | 16 | 17 | 18 | 19 | 20 | 21 | 22 | | 23 | 24 | 25 | 26 | 27 | 28 | 29 | | 30 | 31 |

GOALS **FTW**

MON

9

TUE

10

WED

11

TODAY'S **DO OR DUE:**

VALUES: Who you are

Values represent the things in life that are **important to you:** community service, work ethic, family. Your values reflect who you are and what you do—so it's important to identify the values that shape you. Values can also be applied when determining a major or career path! What values do you want your future career to reflect?

AUG | W T F S S / M T W T F S S / M T W T F S S / M T W T F S S / M T W T F
1 2 3 4 5 / 6 7 8 9 10 11 12 / 13 14 15 16 17 18 19 / 20 21 22 23 24 25 26 / 27 28 29 30 31

2012

TODAY'S **DO OR DUE:**

THUR

12

FRI

13

SAT

14

SUN

15

LOOKING BACK

Check IT!

✓ I totally **aced it**
→ still in **progress**

S / M T W T F S S / M T W T F S S / M T W T F S S / M T W T F S S / M T
1 / 2 3 4 5 6 7 8 / 9 10 11 12 13 14 15 / 16 17 18 19 20 21 22 / 23 24 25 26 27 28 29 / 30 31

GOALS FTW

....
....
....
....
....

TODAY'S **DO OR DUE:**

MON

16

TUE

17

WED

18

QUICK FACTS: Breaking it Down

(Source: www.bc.edu/offices/
careers/step1.html)

Self-Assessment can be explored in four categories:

- **Skills** – Think about skills you have acquired over time.
- **Interests** – Consider what engages you and grabs your attention.
- **Values** – Consider aspects of your life that are of the utmost importance.
- **People & Environment** – Think about the settings and people you
enjoy and work well with.

AUG
W T F S S / M T W T F S S / M T W T F S S / M T W T F S S / M T W T F
1 2 3 4 5 / 6 7 8 9 10 11 12 / 13 14 15 16 17 18 19 / 20 21 22 23 24 25 26 / 27 28 29 30 31

2012

TODAY'S **DO OR DUE:**

THUR

19

Ramadan

FRI

20

SAT

21

SUN

22

LOOKING BACK

Check IT!

✓ I totally **aced it**

→ still in **progress**

THE S / M T W T F S S / M T W T F S S / M T W T F S S / M T W T F S S / M T
1 / 2 3 4 5 6 7 8 / 9 10 11 12 13 14 15 / 16 17 18 19 20 21 22 / 23 24 25 26 27 28 29 / 30 31

GOALS FTW

TODAY'S DO OR DUE:

MON

23

TUE

24

WED

25

Read ON!

Pinpointing a **career path** can be difficult—you're still discovering your academic and personal interests. Look for these titles at your school library to learn more:

• *Gifts Differing: Understanding Personality Type* – Isabel Briggs Myers
• *Self-Assessment Library: Insights into Your Skills, Interests, and Abilities*
   – Stephen P. Robbins
• *Enhancing Learning through Self-Assessment* – David Boud

AUG W T F S S / M T W T F S S / M T W T F S S / M T W T F S S / M T W T F
1 2 3 4 5 / 6 7 8 9 10 11 12 / 13 14 15 16 17 18 19 / 20 21 22 23 24 25 26 / 27 28 29 30 31

2012

TODAY'S **DO OR DUE:**

THUR

26

FRI

27

SAT

28

SUN

29

LOOKING BACK

Check IT!

✓ I totally **aced it**
→ still in **progress**

S / M T W T F S S / M T W T F S S / M T W T F S S / M T
1 / 2 3 4 5 6 7 8 / 9 10 11 12 13 14 15 / 16 17 18 19 20 21 22 / 23 24 25 26 27 28 29 / 30 31

GOALS FTW

TODAY'S DO OR DUE:

MON
30

TUE
31

WED
1
AUG